BODY LANGUAGE
HOW TO READ ANY BODY

BODY LANGUAGE
HOW TO READ
ANY BODY

The Secret To Nonverbal Communication To Understand
& Influence In, Business, Sales, Online, Presenting &
Public Speaking, Healthcare, Attraction & Seduction

DEREK BORTHWICK
Dip.C.Hyp/NLP

DEDICATION

For Skye, Jamie and Adam.

"You see, but you do not observe."

Sherlock Holmes

ABOUT THE AUTHOR

Derek Borthwick, *BSc. (Hons), Dip.C.Hyp/NLP*, has over thirty years of experience in sales, distribution, marketing and has raised over a billion dollars in assets. He has worked with some of the world's largest companies and has lectured at top Scottish Universities. He specialises in advanced communication, persuasion and influence methods. Derek gained a diploma in clinical hypnotherapy and is a certified master practitioner of neurolinguistic programming (NLP). He also has a diploma in organisational and transformation coaching from the Henka Institute.

CONTENTS

**Bonus Chapter And Rapid Learning Accelerator
Audio At The End Of Chapter 22**

PREFACE

"If you want to know what people are really thinking then become more aware."

This is the follow on book from the best-selling book "Inside the Mind of Sales – How to Understand the Mind and Sell Anything." Ever since I first came across nonverbal communication, or body language, at a training seminar in the 1990s, I have been fascinated with the subject and its uses. I wanted to include more on nonverbal communication in the first book, but the vastness of the subject meant that it would have been too much material to incorporate.

For those with a keen interest who want to take this to the next level, this book will serve this purpose. There is a tendency to compartmentalise different skills sets such as sales, negotiating, presenting, etc. Of course, there are structures and steps that you can follow. However, at the heart of success is a sharpened awareness. I was fortunate enough to discover the power of nonverbal communication and body language early in my career. It has fascinated me ever since. I have used these skills that I have learned when selling, during interviews, when coaching, and when public speaking.

There are other books on body language, but for me, there was always something missing. The missing parts to making the picture complete. Many focussed on deciphering the code but didn't focus on what to do next, having read the clues. In this book, we are going to look at how to read and use body language to enhance our communication to persuade and influence people.

I wanted to combine the meanings of the signals with what to do next, depending on the outcome that we want to achieve. I was determined to find those pieces and to see the full picture. This study led me to look at the scientific principles behind body language, nonverbal communication, and the research into advanced persuasion and influence methods. I have combined this, together with my knowledge and expertise of how the mind works and my knowledge of hypnosis and NLP (neurolinguistic programming, which can best be described as software for the mind), together with my coaching skills. This has led to a much deeper understanding of how humans communicate, think and process the world.

In this book, I'm going to share with you the secrets that I have discovered, together with the things that have worked for me over the years. There will be less emphasis on evolutionary interpretations of body language and more on the practical aspects. This book aims to make it useful and practical. I want to share with the reader the principles behind nonverbal communication. This will help the reader discover and be aware of other patterns of behaviour that are not covered. The reader will then be able to interpret the signals using their own observations. For ease of reading, all the scientific research is listed in the references section.

Upon researching and writing this book, I discovered I did some things naturally. However, there were things I had missed and was not aware of. I have had many conversations and instances when lecturing when I referred to nonverbal communication and was surprised to learn that the concept was a major revelation to many.

The key to interpreting nonverbal communication is to start with some guiding principles. For this, we need to understand the workings of the brain and the way people process information. As part of the research, I discovered that to be successful in nonverbal communication, an understanding of advanced communication and sharpened awareness skills are necessary.

I first came across nonverbal communication back in the mid-1990s. I was the manager of an insurance company's sales team and I arranged for us all to go on a training course in Glasgow in Scotland. I was so impressed with the course that I left with an armoury of books and audios. In fact, I still have the original signed books to this day! Having bought the material, I then set about studying it and found it to be an eye opener. This really helped me in my sales and management career. Later on during my study and research into hypnosis and NLP (neurolinguistic programming) it became apparent that to be a great hypnotist you had to have a sharpened awareness. This also includes a solid knowledge of nonverbal communication to set up an effective biofeedback loop. This fascination has stayed with me to this day.

My research has taken me into the world of nonverbal communication, body language, clinical hypnosis, stage hypnosis, neurolinguistic programming (NLP), neuroscience, and the world of persuasion and influence. Combining these disciplines, together with the published material relating to nonverbal communication and my own extensive experience, has allowed me to develop something very special.

Simply follow the principles in this book, together with the breakdown of patterns of behaviour, to ensure your success. This will not only transform your business, professional and sales life but also your personal, family and intimate relationships. We will combine both conscious and unconscious learning uniquely. The book will address conscious learning. The audio program will focus on unconscious learning and will help program your mind for success. These methods and processes are very powerful and work.

They literally will transform the way that you read people. I truly believe that this is the most complete nonverbal and body language approach.

HOW TO USE THIS BOOK

This book is divided into 2 parts.

Part one

Part one covers how the brain, the nervous system and the mind work, together with the principles for deciphering nonverbal communication. The principles are the real secret to being successful in any form of communication and analysis. The main patterns of body language have been broken down and then analysed to help you learn these signals. It is important to return to this part as needed.

Part two

Part two consists of applying the patterns of nonverbal communication to assist you in persuading and influencing people across a range of situations and disciplines.

Your bonus

The real secret to interpreting body language comes from a sharpened awareness. To help with this, there is a bonus Rapid Learning Accelerator Audio Program, which will help program your mind for success and is available to all readers. **(See the**

end of Chapter 22) The changes from this will be subtle, ongoing and will be below your level of awareness. I recommend you use earphones when listening to the track. The best time to use this recording is before going to sleep at night, or during a quiet period during the day when you will not be disturbed. Use the audio as often as you can. Ideally, this should be once a day for 30 days.

This audio is very powerful.
Do not use this track when driving, operating any machinery or when you need to be fully alert.

There is also a bonus chapter "Seating For Power & Influence."

The journey is not the trip

There is a lot of information in this book. It is best to view this as an ongoing development plan. You can refine your skills as you go along. Make sure to read the first part of the book carefully before moving to the second part. The principles discussed in this book will massively improve your communication skills across the range of your business, personal, family, and intimate communications. Let's make it fun. I'm excited to begin, so let's get started.

PART ONE

The Mind Body Connection

To Receive Your Complimentary Rapid Learning Accelerator Audio and Bonus Chapter "Seating For Power & Influence," Go To The End of Chapter 22

CHAPTER 1

Inner Thoughts & Outer Expressions

Before we explore body language, let's agree upon some definitions. This will aid us in our understanding and will provide us with a reference going forward.

Body language

"The gestures, movements, and mannerisms by which a person or animal communicates with others"
Merriam Webster Dictionary

Nonverbal communication

There is not a dictionary definition for nonverbal communication. For the purpose of this book, we will describe this as "communication that is other than verbal."

More than just the body

We are communicating all the time. We just can't not communicate. Even the act of not communicating is the act of communication! We communicate not just with our words and our voice, but through tone, volume, expression and nonverbal communication. Nonverbal communication is not just confined to body language. We express this through the environment that we create for ourselves. This can be seen through the clothes that we wear, our choice of accessories, where we choose to live, together with our choice of furnishings. These and more all communicate a message. Combining both body language and nonverbal communication gives us a much stronger base upon which to gain a greater understanding of others. In this book, the approach that we are going to adopt is twofold.

The first part is to analyse body language and nonverbal communication to give us a greater understanding.

The second part is to discover how we can use this understanding of nonverbal and body language to communicate our message better. We can use this very powerful method to influence people to get more of what we want.

Why bother to learn body language?

There is a strong link between the mind body connection, and we can use this principle. Many successful actors can fake a mood by getting themselves into the required frame of mind. They then let their faces and body do the rest naturally. We will look at this principle in more detail later when looking at how to use nonverbal communication and body language to influence people.

Repetition

It has been estimated by psychologists that habits account for around 40% of what we do and that as much as 95% of what we experience is below conscious awareness. Many movements, gestures and postures have been performed thousands of times before. Think about interlocking your fingers. If I asked you which thumb was on top, most people would struggle to know the answer without doing it. We can use this act of unconscious repetition of behaviours to help us identify patterns of nonverbal communication. The beauty of this is that most of it takes place beneath people's conscious awareness. This means that it has not been controlled.

Many people may consciously try to conceal insecurities or weaknesses, but these are difficult to cover up. They leak the signals. Therefore, the more that we can read patterns of body language and nonverbal communication, then the more control and confidence we will have when communicating with others.

Ethical or manipulation

When we hear about body language, it conjures up different images, from suspicion to fascination, together with ethical questions. My view is that anything that can improve communication between two or more people has got to be a good thing. Being able to read body language can help in business, management, coaching and sales. It can also help in the medical and dental professions, therapy, sport together with our personal and intimate relationships. Yet no one teaches us this. There are very few scenarios where a sharpened awareness of body language or nonverbal communication cannot be used for real benefit.

Some of us may think of manipulative people. We may even wonder if they are trying to manipulate us. Of course, this is a possibility. Therefore, it is worthwhile spending time to recognise and decode nonverbal and body language clues. This means that if someone is trying to manipulate us, this will give us an advantage and help us to read those signals.

We will look at how we can use body language and nonverbal communication to build rapport and influence people in the second part of the book.

Is it easy to learn?

We already know how to read body language. If someone ran towards us with an angry expression on their face waving a sword, we would interpret this as a threatening event. Many of us will have detected our boss or partner may be in a bad mood, just by observing their actions. We have all had that moment when we have realised that perhaps it is not a good time to raise a particular topic. Everyone can therefore read body language, but it is the degree to which we can read some of the more subtle aspects that differentiate us.

Learning body language is like any new skill. If you have ever tried to learn a new sport or to learn a musical instrument, at first, it can seem quite daunting. Then, as you practise, it becomes easier. The best way to learn body language is to break it down into smaller chunks. Many of you will be familiar with the chocolate or candy bar the Toblerone. The Toblerone is made of very hard chocolate. However, if we try to eat it all at once, it would be very difficult. The triangular hard chocolate causes pain in our mouths when bitten. However, if it is broken down into chunks, then it becomes much more manageable. This serves as a good metaphor. Before we look at the principles of how we can develop the skills of interpreting body language, let's look at first how we learn.

If you want to be more successful in life, then sharpen your awareness. We can learn to sharpen our awareness and combine this with some conscious learning patterns. This will give us all the ingredients for success. Let's look now at how we can do this by first learning about awareness.

THE LIMITS OF OUR ATTENTION

George Miller, a cognitive psychologist, published a paper in 1956. It is often used to argue the case that the human mind can hold 7 plus or minus 2 pieces of information in conscious awareness. The 7 plus or minus 2 model serves as a good metaphor, but it is more complicated than this. We have a limit to how much information we can process consciously before we get confused. For example, you are now aware of your left foot, the feeling of your right hand, and the clothes that you are wearing. These things were already taking place and the sensory data was being processed, but unconsciously. If, for example, some liquid drips onto your clothes, the moment that you feel wet, this would be raised to consciousness. This feeling would be important and would be raised to consciousness for you to analyse and process.

Our limited capacity for awareness (7 plus or minus 2 pieces of information) or limited bandwidth means it is difficult to do many things at once. I like to think of the brain as a computer. When using our computers, the more programs that are running then the slower that the computer will run. Similarly, this means that if the brain is overloaded, then the harder it becomes to observe things until eventually it crashes. Hypnotists and pickpockets exploit this limited brain bandwidth by using overload and confusion techniques that distract attention.

The biggest mistake

The biggest mistake that novices make when learning and analysing body language is to look at gestures in isolation. They are so intent on looking at one piece of body expression that they miss out on what is really going on. It's very similar to how a magician directs you to look at one hand. While you are looking at the directed hand, you miss out on what is going on with the other hand. Human communication is complicated and the best way to analyse body language is to use the principle of stacking.

Stacking the deck

To describe stacking, let's use an example. Consider taking a piece of paper and placing it on a table. If we were to blow on it, the piece of paper would move easily. The foundations are not strong. However, if we were to add further pieces of paper to the pile, it would become harder to blow. Eventually, we would not be able to blow the pieces of paper and make them move. It would have a solid foundation. The same principle applies when analysing body language or nonverbal communication. The more pieces that reinforce your observations then the stronger is the conclusion.

CHAPTER 2

The Command Centre

To understand the principles discussed in the following chapters and how they will help you master the reading of body language, we must look at the workings of the mind and brain.

The brain acts as a predictive mechanism. It is constantly analysing the environment. It compares the environment that we find ourselves in, against what it predicts that the environment should be like. If the environment is not as predicted, then this is raised to consciousness and processed. Think about walking down the street in your everyday life. You won't remember most of the people that you encounter, except the very attractive person, the unusual looking person, or someone displaying unusual behaviour. This is because this ties in with the model that the brain expects to experience. There is no need to involve the critical brain for things that are predicted when it could be used for thinking elsewhere.

Let's just suppose that you suddenly see somebody walking towards you wearing a clown's outfit. This would be classed as unusual. It would not be as predicted and would be raised to consciousness. The same thing occurs if you see an attractive person, a person who looks unusual or someone who is behaving oddly. This principle is worth remembering. We must look at how an individual reacts to their perception of the environment and not how we think they should react. Let's move on now to some brain basics.

THE THREE BRAIN BASICS

We have three "brains," with each performing specialised functions. Fig.1 This three brain model became known as the "triune model" from the work of Paul MacLean. While there have been further refinements, it serves as a good metaphor.

The three brains are:

1. Reptilian, stem brain or paleocortex.
2. Mammalian, midbrain, or limbic system (chimp brain).
3. Human or neocortex brain.

Understanding the triune

The reptilian brain or paleocortex filters all the incoming messages and handles most of the fight, flight or freeze responses. It is also responsible for some of the very basic and strong primitive emotions. Its prime responsibility is not with thinking, but with survival. When driving a car, if somebody suddenly jumps out in front of the car, we don't want to think about applying the brakes. It's done automatically for us by the reptilian brain, and with it comes the outer expressions.

The midbrain, also known as the mammalian brain or the limbic system, is sometimes referred to as the chimp brain. It makes sense of social situations, attaches meaning to situations and is the emotional centre. The midbrain or chimp brain is the honest part of the brain. It leaks the real thoughts that may be suppressed through non-verbal activity, which we can interpret.

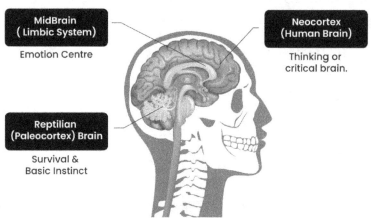

**MidBrain
(Limbic System)**

Emotion Centre

**Neocortex
(Human Brain)**

Thinking or
critical brain.

**Reptilian
(Paleocortex) Brain**

Survival &
Basic Instinct

Fig.1

The neocortex is the outer part of the brain responsible for critical thinking and logic. It analyses things. It will critique and analyse a proposition or proposal. It is your lying brain and will justify your behaviour, however irrational. Information has to pass through the reptilian brain, to the midbrain and onto the neocortex to be analysed and critiqued. Let's use an example of how the three brains might work.

Imagine that somebody appears wearing an outfit that is shocking, inappropriate and not to your taste. The reptilian brain immediately processes this unexpected and unpredicted change as a mild shock. The limbic brain then puts context to this shocking outfit and creates an emotion. This may be disbelief, shock, horror or even humour. The neocortex then analyses the information, and the inner voice may say, "Do they not have a mirror in their house?"

The neocortex attempts to protect us and the other person, as harsh truths can offend. It may cause us to lie to avoid losing a friendship by protecting others' feelings. The neocortex has worked out that the lie is beneficial to us. However, our true thoughts are leaked nonverbally. We may say,

"I love your new outfit. It really suits you!"

However, this may not be what we are thinking? In business, we may say to our boss,

"I really like the new sales strategy for our company. It sounds very exciting."

However, do we mean it? If we are saying this to others, would it be fair to assume that they may be saying this about us too? The neocortex is thus the lying brain. It also justifies our behaviour. For example,

"It doesn't matter if I steal from them, as they have plenty of money, anyway."

Remember, for something to be interpreted as true, it does not have to be true, just plausible. This is important. Each of us has our version of reality. We construct this by the brain filtering the data coming into our brain through the primary senses. All data is generalised, distorted, some are deleted and we form our reality from this. We never actually experience full reality, just our version of it. This is our map of the world. This explains why we all like different music, food and holidays or vacations.

We are going to use this knowledge of how the brain works to establish the fundamental principles. These principles will help us decode the body language and the nonverbal communication that we encounter daily.

This will be explored in greater detail in the next chapter. For more detail on how the mind and brain work, the reader is referred to the publication, "Inside the Mind of Sales – How to Understand the Mind and Sell Anything" by the author.

SHARPENING AWARENESS

Sharpening up

Like everything in communication, whether in sales, counselling, coaching, dealing with clients or patients, the more that you can sharpen your awareness, then the more successful you will be.

Our brain can only process a limited number of things at one time. We need to make sure that we have as many of these focused on external awareness and observation as possible.

Internal & external worlds

We have our external reality, which we perceive in near to real time. We also have an imagined or recalled reality. Our representational systems are used to code our version of reality.

The representational systems are:

Visual - Images
Auditory - Sounds
Auditory Digital - Talking to yourself
Kinaesthetic - Feelings
Olfactory - Smell
Gustatory – Taste

This then gives us our map. This map is unique to us. Imagine going on holiday. Each of us pays attention to different things. Two people going on an identical holiday would have a different map or story to tell from it. For some, it may be too hot, while for others it may not be hot enough. Some may love the hotel, others less so.

By knowing how people react to a real event, we can understand how they would react to an imagined event. In other words, the thoughts that people are experiencing in their head, or what they are thinking about, will be expressed externally. Let's look at an example from the "Inside the Mind of Sales" book.

Being a lemon

I'd like you to think about a lemon and to imagine holding that lemon in your hand. Notice the bright yellow colour and firmness of the lemon as you gently squeeze it, feeling its waxy surface. Bring the lemon slowly up to your nose, breathe in and noticed that faint smell of lemon. Now take the lemon and place it on a cutting board. Reach across, and grab a very sharp knife. Begin slowly slicing the lemon gently with the knife and notice how the lemon juice drips gently out from the lemon. You may even hear a sound as the lemon juice escapes. Notice the fresh clean smell of lemon as you breathe in. Keep on cutting so that the lemon becomes in two halves. Now, cut a wedge of lemon. Reach down and grab the wedge of lemon and bring it slowly up to your nose. Notice how the smell of lemon gets stronger and stronger the closer that it gets to your nose. Continue bringing the lemon to your nose. Breathe in the fresh, pleasing lemon smell. Now take the lemon and open your mouth and take a big bite.

Many of you will now be salivating. When I have described

Fig 2

and used the same story in front of a live audience, many screw their faces up when imagining taking a bite from the imaginary lemon. Of course, there is no lemon. It is purely imaginary. Many of you may have salivated and some of you may even have screwed your face up in anticipation. This shows the power of imagination. There was no lemon, but you engaged your internal thoughts and had an external reaction. This is important as we express what we are thinking through our external expressions relating to those representational systems. (Fig.2)

STATE SECRETS

I cannot emphasise enough how important managing our state is. The ability to manage our state is one of the key skills that any communicator needs to do. I am sure that we have all witnessed when the attitude of somebody was less than favourable. This attitude rubs off on us and affects our engagement with them. It has been said that enthusiasm is infectious. It works the other way too.

Fluidity of State

Being able to move into different states of mind takes a bit of practice. This is something that you can practise away from interactions with people.

People often say that it is not possible to change your state. Yet is this not what actors do when they get into character, or when a rock star goes on stage? Imagine winning the lottery. Do you think that your mental state would change? Is that not what we did when you imagined biting into the lemon? The emotional state changed and there was a nonverbal response.

The easiest way to get into a particular state is to revivify a previous experience strongly and realistically. The secret to the success of this is imagination. It is the same part of the brain that processes something vividly imagined, that processes something real. Let's experiment with this. Pick a time when there are no distractions and immerse yourself as much as you can in the following exercise. You may even want to close your eyes to enhance the experience.

CONTROLLING THE STATE

Let's take the principles of state control and use them to create the desired state. This takes a bit of practice. The more you do it, the better you will get at it. Let's start.

First, close your eyes and think about a time when you were at your most invincible, your most confident and very best. Make the experience as big as an IMAX screen. Remember to experience this as if reliving the experience and seeing it through your own eyes and not sitting in the audience watching. Make the colours bright and bold and turn up the brightness in the image. See what you saw, hear what you heard, feel what you were feeling. Taste what you may have tasted and smell what you may have smelt. As the images, sounds, smells, feelings and tastes start to come back, imagine that there is a dial right in front of you labelled "experience enhancer." Imagine turning that dial to full. Notice how the feelings intensify and hold the state for about two minutes.

Now open your eyes and think about something fairly ordinary and mundane like, what did you have for your dinner last night? Let's repeat the exercise and this time let's really intensify the experience. Repeat the exercise. Do it again and again.

Every time we repeat this, which is called fractionation, it deepens the experience. Depending on your level of absorption, will determine how differently you feel when you open your eyes and return to normal. The key to this is to be playful and to resist the temptation to be too logical and literal. The more that you practise, the better that you will become. Remember to be playful.

People are shifting states all the time. You may have noticed the change as you went through the exercise. A smile may have appeared on your face. Well, the same thing is happening with people when they are imagining things. Signals are being leaked.

Tips for Practicing

There is a tendency, for some, if they are very logical and structured, to try and force the experience. The key to success is not to try. Just let it happen and be playful. The act of trying often hinders progress. The key to state management is to be immersed in the experience. The brighter and clearer the picture and the more senses that are involved in the experience, then the more vivid the recall of the state becomes. Think "be playful" and just roll with it.

REAL OR IMAGINED

Whenever you are learning a new skill, it can take time to master it. However, proper practice will get you there. As discussed, something that is vividly imagined and something real are both processed by the same parts of the brain. Could it be possible to imagine a way to succeed? Let's have a look at what the research says.

Really?

A study from the Journal of Physiology in 1995 had volunteers play a simple sequence of piano notes each day for five consecutive days. Their brains were scanned each day in the region connected to the finger muscles. Another set of volunteers was asked to imagine playing the notes instead. They also had their brains scanned each day. It could be seen that the changes in the brain in those who imagined playing piano notes were the same as those who actually played the piano. This shows that the brain doesn't distinguish real from imaginary!

LEARNING TO LEARN

Many people expect to master a skill too quickly. Let's look at how we learn and, in the next chapter, we will start the learning process.

We have two minds, the conscious and the unconscious mind. The unconscious mind is sometimes referred to as the subconscious mind. Let's look at the two minds in more detail.

The conscious mind

The conscious mind is the rational and critical part of the mind. It controls "willpower" and short-term memory together with analysing our internal thoughts. It also runs an internal check on the information that is coming in and compares this with what we believe to be true. If the information matches what we believe to be true, the belief is reinforced. If the information contradicts what is believed, then the new suggestion is rejected, and no change in behaviour or beliefs occurs.

The unconscious mind

The unconscious mind is over a million times more powerful than the conscious mind, according to Dr. Bruce Lipton. Think of the conscious mind as the driver of the bus and the unconscious mind as the bus. The conscious mind directs the bus in the direction that we want to go. The unconscious mind controls the engine and all the moving parts. The unconscious mind has a limited ability to make judgements, and it relies on the critical factor within the conscious mind to do this. The unconscious mind also regulates breathing, blood pressure, heartbeat, together with many other unconscious processes. It controls our habits, behaviours and its job is to keep us safe.

The four stages of learning

As we learn and develop, the unconscious mind takes over more and more of the learning. When learning a new skill, we go through four stages of learning and these are listed below.

1. Unconscious Incompetence. We are unaware that we don't know how to do something.

2. Conscious Incompetence. We are aware that we don't know how to do something.

3. Conscious Competence. We can now do something but must concentrate, and it is not yet natural.

4. Unconscious Competence. The skill is now hard wired and we can do it without thinking.

Learning from chicken sexers

Learning occurs with repetition and this can be illustrated by chicken sexers. Separating the egg-producing female from male chicks has important commercial value and is a skill called "sexing." The best chicken sexers come from Japan. Separating males from females is difficult, as both look identical to the untrained eye. The training method involves training the brain through trial and error until it becomes an unconscious process. Something that can seem impossible, to begin with, soon becomes an unconscious, competent process.

When learning a new skill, it is important to realise the four stages of learning. When going through this book, there may be elements of body language that you are aware of and that you do well. There will be other things that you are not aware of.

The key is to break things down and practice them. Trying to learn everything all at once can cause a feeling of being overwhelmed. When you first learnt a new skill, like learning to ride a bike or learning to juggle, there was a point where you didn't know what was happening. A moment occurred where it was happening all by itself and it just got smoother and smoother as time went. Work your way through the book, paying particular attention to awareness. Practice as often as possible and in as many environments as you can.

CHAPTER 3

Getting Started

I am sure that you are eager to get started deciphering body language and nonverbal signals. Let's start right from the basics. In this chapter, we will be exploring key principles that you can use to spot other patterns of behaviour that may not be covered. Being able to read body language can lighten up even the dullest meeting or social interaction.

FIRST PRINCIPLES

The first step in body language and nonverbal analysis is to shift the focus of awareness from internal to external. This means shifting from the little voice internally, which is thinking what we are going to say next, to one of observation. This also means paying more attention to what we see and less to internal images. The mindset that we want to adopt is one of genuine curiosity. I find body language and nonverbal communication fascinating, fun and entertaining.

Some people find it easier than others to quieten their mind and to shift to a heightened external awareness. Listening to the

Bonus Rapid Learning Accelerator Audio that comes with the book will help you with this. Let's look at how we can do this.

LOOKING AROUND

Step one

The first step is to start looking around you and paying attention to what you see. Go for a walk if possible and really start looking and noticing things. If you can go out and look around you wherever you are. Your challenge is to stay in up-time and to quieten the inner voice. Start describing what you see and what do you hear. Is there a particular aroma in the air? How warm is the air? How are you feeling about the experience? Say this out loud and this will keep you in uptime.

This may seem very basic, and there is a temptation to skip this step. Do not skip this step. To become good at reading body language, you must get good at being in the moment and being in up-time. Those who can control their minds, such as Yogis, practice quietening their mind for hours on end. We don't need to go that far. We are not wanting to clear our minds, but to train our awareness to refocus on external events. The key to being a successful communicator, and being able to persuade and influence people, is by having a sharpened awareness.

Keep practising this and start to notice things. Try to notice as much as you can by using all your senses. Make it a habit by practising regularly. If you skip this and don't practice this step, then it is like looking through binoculars that have dirty lenses. You won't see anything clearly. Once you learn and train your mind to focus externally, you will be surprised at what you notice.

Step two

The next step is to start observing people that you don't know. Try to gain as much information as you can about that person just by looking at them. Have a guess. Observe how they walk. How do they carry themselves? How fast are they walking? Do they look tense or relaxed? Are they looking up or are they looking down? What do their clothes tell you? What do their accessories tell you? If you are observing two or more people interacting, what does the interaction look like? Do they look like they get on? Are they close? Who is the dominant person in the relationship?

There is a lot of information that can be gleaned just by sharpening your awareness. The point here is not to judge people, but merely to get an impression of what they are likely to be like. We will not always be correct, but this is the first step in learning to sharpen our awareness. Get into the habit of people watching and get curious. Think of it as a puzzle. You are trying to get as much information as you can about that person without actually speaking to them.

Don't worry if this all seems daunting and if you're not able to spot the clues. By the time you have finished this book, you will have a thorough understanding of reading body language and how to use it to influence other people. Let's begin.

CHAPTER 4

Seven Secret Principles

We are now setting the foundations and practices in motion to gain an understanding of the mind. Let's now explore the principles that will unlock the secrets to understanding body language and nonverbal communication.

PHYSIOLOGY AND PSYCHOLOGY

When people are in an emotionally charged state, their body language reflects this. The big question is, could your physical actions affect your emotions?

The psychologist Amy Cuddy found that there is a strong link between feelings of power and adopting a power pose. It is not surprising that this takes place because other disciplines, such as yoga, have body positions at their core.

This means that by adopting a different body posture, it is possible to generate a corresponding emotional response. You may have noticed that when somebody is depressed, they look down at the ground and make themselves smaller. Someone who has just had a winning or a victorious moment will often look up, and you may see a clenching or pumping of the fists as they make themselves bigger. This is the body language of victory and success.

The key to our success in reading body language is by reading emotions and feelings that are generated and leaked. These emotions and feelings are expressed through body language.

ACTIONS SPEAK LOUDER THAN WORDS

Seven powerful principles

- *The outer expression is a reflection of the inner thought.*

- *The stronger the emotion, the stronger the body language.*

- *People display signs of comfort or discomfort, tension or relaxation.*

- *People move towards things that they like and away from things that they dislike.*

- *Upward gestures indicate positivity, downward gestures indicate the opposite.*

- *People look at things that they like and look away from things that they don't.*

- *Stacked gestures are more powerful than isolated gestures.*

Let's look at these principles in more detail.

PRINCIPLE 1

"The outer expression is a reflection of inner thought."

Human beings are communication machines. We just can't not communicate. Even the act of not communicating is an act of communication. We can all read body language it's just the degree to which we can do it.

Let's take an extreme example of the principle of the outer expression reflecting the inner thought. Think about somebody who is very angry. What sort of behaviours would they typically exhibit? They would be unlikely to be smiling and they may be snarling. We may hear them shouting and an expression of anger on their face and a lowering of the eyebrows.

In this very simple example, we know, without listening to any of the words, that they may say that they are in an angry state. As the state is one of anger, then the body reflects this state. This principle is key to understanding and is worth remembering.

PRINCIPLE 2

"The stronger the emotion, the stronger the body language."

Extreme anger is easy to spot. However, there are degrees of emotions. It becomes harder to spot mild annoyance, but the signs are still there for the trained eye.

These feelings and emotions are leaked from the limbic system, or chimp brain, and the reptilian brain or paleocortex. They are expressed through body language and non-verbal communication. Let's understand these in a bit more detail.

Understanding the Reptile Brain

The reptilian brain works based on:

- *Is something a threat or a danger?*

- *Is something new and exciting?*
- *If it is new, get to the point quickly and make it simple.*

What does this mean for body language?

- *Displays of feeling threatened or discomfort.*
- *Displays of boredom or disinterest.*
- *Displays of confusion or annoyance.*

Working with the reptile and the chimp

While the neocortex or critical brain focuses on critique and evaluation, the currency of the limbic system (chimp brain) and the reptilian brain is emotions and feelings.

PRINCIPLE 3

"We react either with a display of comfort or discomfort."

Displays of comfort

Think about someone who is in a very comfortable position. Let's consider a situation where we could observe this. It may be observing someone sunbathing on the beach in a warm, beautiful setting. What might we observe that indicates comfort.

The muscles of their body would be relaxed. We can see this in the facial muscles and the neck. These often carry a lot of tension. We would see the arms and the hands are relaxed too. The breathing is likely to be slower and deeper.

Displays of discomfort

Let's think about a situation where people would exhibit feelings of discomfort. Perhaps it may be at a busy airport with lots of flight delays and cancellations. We would see the tension in the face muscles and perhaps some tension in the upper shoulders, neck and back. There may be some fidgeting going on, and the arms and hands exhibit movement or tension. The breathing is likely to be shallow, high in the chest and faster.

Signs of nerves

Many processes are carried out, beneath our level of awareness automatically, by the autonomic nervous system. The autonomic nervous system regulates bodily functions such as heart rate, blood pressure, pupil dilation, body temperature, sweating, and digestion. There are only two processes that can be consciously overridden without training. One is the blink rate and the other breathing.

Two nerve centres

Within the autonomic nervous system, there are two systems responsible for regulating the organs of the body in response to a stimulus. (Fig.3) These are the parasympathetic nervous system and the sympathetic nervous system. The hypothalamus in the brain maintains homeostasis or balance between these two nervous systems.

The parasympathetic nervous system is stimulated when we are at rest, "the rest and digest state." The sympathetic nervous system is stimulated by the fear response at times of stress. The amygdala sends a message to the hypothalamus. If overstimulated, it triggers the fight, flight, or freeze response. This prepares the body for fight or flight by increasing the blood flow to the large muscles and away from the extremities. Breathing becomes shallower, faster, higher, in the chest, and the heart rate increases. Non-essential systems shut down and peripheral vision together with hearing are reduced. We experience tunnel or foveal vision, and the digestive and immune systems shut down. This causes butterflies in the stomach. Blood drains from the prefrontal cortex, shutting down rational thought. This makes it virtually impossible to learn anything or to focus on small things. It also makes it difficult to engage with other people, as the survival instincts kick in.

Homeostasis Is the Balance Between the Parasympathetic and Sympathetic Nervous System.

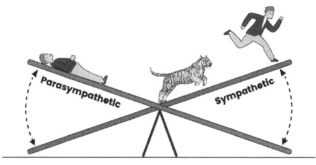

Rest, Heal and Digest –
Parasympathetic Nervous
System Stimulated

Fight, Flight or Freeze –
Sympathetic Nervous
System Stimulated

Fig.3

Many of us will have had the experience of being under stress and trying to read a page in a book. We can read a passage over and over and it just won't go in. Think about a heated argument that you have had where you didn't say the right things at the time. Then afterwards, as you cool down, thoughts of "I wish I had said that" occur. Why does this happen? This is because you were not thinking critically. Now that we know what happens when somebody is stressed or nervous, we can observe the changes.

When in the resting stage, blood flow to the extremities increases. This causes a more flushed look on the face, a fuller lower lip and deeper slower breathing. The pupils will be less dilated to allow for a wider field of view. If shaking hands with someone, the hand is often warm and not moist.

Compare this with someone nervous or stressed and there is less colour in the face. The language again reflects this with the expression "white as a ghost." Breathing is shallower and higher in the chest, and the lower lip is less full and paler. The hands are often cold to the touch and may be moist too.

These are some of the more advanced observations and we don't have to focus on all of these, but it shows that there is a link between thoughts and external expression physiologically.

PRINCIPLE 4

"People move towards things that they like and away from things that they dislike."

Think about an everyday occurrence. If there is someone that we don't like, we will try to avoid them. In many cases, people will avoid going to the same venues as that person. In a business environment, people will tend to sit as far apart from each other as they can. In a networking event, they may occupy different areas of a room. On the contrary, people who like each other will sit next to each other. In body language terms, leaning or moving towards something can indicate a liking or interest, while the converse can apply. The phrase "I just couldn't even bear to be in the same room as him" gives us a clue.

We have space around us that we feel comfortable with. (Fig 4.)

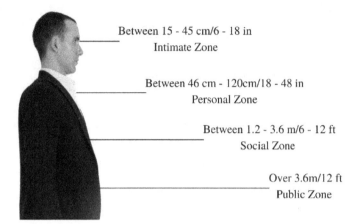

Between 15 - 45 cm/6 - 18 in
Intimate Zone

Between 46 cm - 120cm/18 - 48 in
Personal Zone

Between 1.2 - 3.6 m/6 - 12 ft
Social Zone

Over 3.6m/12 ft
Public Zone

Fig.4

Getting too close to someone's space can cause someone to move back to maintain a comfortable space. I remember once being in a meeting with a client where my colleague kept getting too close. I could see the client moving backwards in the room as my colleague kept trying to get closer. The client's personal space was being invaded. As people start getting to know each other, this space decreases and becomes obvious in an intimate relationship.

PRINCIPLE 5

Upward gestures indicate positivity, downward gestures indicate the opposite.

When people are in a positive state, then we see gravity defying or upward gestures. The phrase "things are looking up gives us a clue." Think about someone who is depressed. The shoulders are down. The head is down and they look down. The arms are hanging down too. Now think about a successful athlete who has just won a race. The hands and arms may be raised and often the head is tilted head back looking up.

PRINCIPLE 6

"People look at things that they like and look away from things that they don't."

When we see something that we like, we look at it more often and for longer. We will explore this later in the book. The language again gives us a clue. "I just couldn't bear to look at her." If we have just seen something that we shouldn't have or that is horrific, many people just look away.

PRINCIPLE 7

"Stacked gestures are more powerful than isolated gestures."

This is a very powerful principle and is the part where most people have a problem with body language. A gesture in isolation does not give us enough information to come to a conclusion. It is merely a clue. Further gestures that are congruent with the original gesture will help reinforce your conclusion. The more congruent the gestures are then the more accurate our conclusion is likely to be.

Imagine we were investigating a crime. If someone does not have an alibi does not make them guilty, but equally, it does not make them innocent!

CHAPTER 5

Talking Legs & Feet

The feet and legs are regarded as the most honest part of the body and yet many of us just focus on the face. We have had lots of practice reading the face. Most people are aware of how important and powerful facial communication is. Many of us have learned to control this to some extent. We are least aware of what we are doing with our legs and feet. Consequently, they give away a lot of unconscious signals. We have more control over our hands and arms, largely because we can see them as they move around. Less so with our feet and legs unless we look down. If you want to gain some clues about people's inner world, focus on the legs and feet.

FEET

Let's begin with the feet. The feet are the furthest away from our head. We often pay little attention to them and, most times, we are blissfully unaware of what they are doing.

I once worked with somebody in an office and sat opposite. While sitting opposite, I realised a periodic thumping noise. The thump was random, and it did not have any form of rhythm or pattern to it. It took me a while to work out that this noise was coming from my co-worker banging the floor with their foot. This person was blissfully unaware of what they were doing. For them, it was a display of comfort. It was quite off-putting, but I never raised it with them.

Foot tappers and pointers

Sometimes we may see foot tapping from someone who appears to be listening intently. This can often indicate a sign of discomfort. It can also indicate nervousness if coupled with the vibrating knee. You may observe a small foot jab while other parts of the body remain in control. This may indicate discomfort and that the person does not agree with what you are saying.

Attractive feet

Fig.5

The feet point towards the person who we find the most appealing and attractive. (Fig.5) This can occur both in a standing and seated environment. Let's assume that there is a group of men standing in the company of an attractive woman. If the men find the woman attractive, then the feet or a foot will point towards her. If a more attractive woman comes and joins the group, the dynamic may change and the feet may point towards to new arrival. The previous woman will detect this and may either leave the group or her body language will reflect this change of attention.

Dominant feet

The feet point to the person that is the most dominant in a group. Consider a group of people when they first gather together. A lot of hustling establishes who is the alpha within the group. Once established, everybody falls into line and knows their place..

When you say something that is interesting and which has an immediate benefit to the person to whom you are speaking, feet and body position alter. If their feet and body were not previously pointing at you, they will start to. However, remember there has to be something in it for them, either something interesting or a benefit. Telling them a secret works well!

Happy feet

We have already seen that the outer expression reflects the inner thought. Think about what happens when somebody is happy and excited. The feet and legs become more active. The phrase "she jumped for joy," gives us a clue. When emotions are high, we see people dancing with joy and young children skipping with joy.

Some people even engage in their dance routine. You may have witnessed this on television shows when people have won a substantial amount of money. We also see this when a football or soccer player scores a goal.

Compare this with a sad and sombre occasion such as a funeral. In this setting, very little active foot movement is displayed. Someone comfortable and relaxed in their environment may display some foot movement. While sometimes obscured under a non-transparent table, there is often upper body movement to reflect this.

Fig.6

Happy feet are "dancing feet." (Fig.6) People may display foot movement when seated, which takes the form of an up and down movement. It is important to differentiate between "dancing feet" and a nervous display. The nervous display is a quick up and down movement of the foot linked to leg movement and the vibrating knee. The vibrating knee can be a sign of nervousness, excitement, or impatience. Often vibration in the upper body is seen. To understand the exact meaning other nonverbal cues need to be examined. Sometimes dancing feet indicate frustration and impatience. This sometimes occurs when listening to somebody that you wish would speed up a bit and get to the point.

Kicking feet

The language again gives us a clue. You may have heard the expression, "I could have kicked myself." This gives an indication that frustration or discomfort is being experienced. We may hear or doing something that we don't want to and our feet want to kick out. (Fig.7)

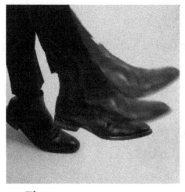

Fig.7

In the modern environment, it is unacceptable to go around kicking people. In cases of extreme anger, people may lash out and kick at things and sometimes other people. We also see kicking feet when people are sitting down with their legs crossed. Foot movement will either be pivoting at the ankle up and down or there will be a front to back small kicking motion. (Fig.7) It is worth paying attention to this unconscious activity. It can indicate discomfort and or disagreement.

Positive feet

Fig.8

When we feel positive about something, we stand tall and look up. The language gives us a clue again. "Things are looking up." When we say that things are looking up, it has positive connotations. We see this when someone points their foot in the air. (Fig.8) This is more obvious when someone is standing.

Negative feet

When we don't like something, our feet will point down and the toes will curl. The clue comes from the language. You may have

Fig.9

heard the expression "toe-curling." It indicates an unpleasant experience, annoyance, or embarrassment. For example, "Just thinking about my ex-boyfriend makes my toes curl."

In most situations, we won't witness toes curling but we can observe a pointing down of the foot. (Fig.9)

As with everything in body language, we need a base line. Consider speaking to someone who has their legs crossed and their foot dancing up and down. We then ask a question and suddenly their foot stops dancing. It then swivels from the ankle and points down. This could indicate a toe-curling moment.

Welcoming feet

Fig.10

Consider meeting someone for the first time and they are not in a hurry. The handshake and smile may appear genuine. (Chapter 6) However, if they just swivel their head towards you and their feet do not point in your direction, this could indicate a lack of genuine interest. It may suggest wanting to be left alone or being busy. The distance that somebody keeps their feet away from you can indicate the warmth of the welcome. (Fig.10) Someone who keeps their feet at a distance and bends towards you may indicate that they don't wish to get close to you. This can also occur if someone is from a geographical area or culture where more space is acceptable.

Goodbye feet

When most people communicate in a business environment, they tend to communicate face on. Their feet and toes point at

each other. When somebody wants to indicate that the meeting is over, one foot may turn and point in the direction that they wish to go. (Fig.11) A stronger indication is that both feet will point in the direction that somebody wants to go. If you are speaking to somebody and they are in a hurry or want to be somewhere else, you may notice that their head looks at you, while the feet point in the direction that they wish to go in.

Fig.11

"I really must go!"

If they really want to go somewhere, their torso will also point to where they wish to go. You may notice the angle of the torso beginning to increase as they turn away from you. (Fig.12) This may be subtle. This is often not a good time to discuss an important matter with somebody. Mentioning this and saying that "I sense that this is not a good time," will gain you kudos.

I once worked in an office with somebody who had very low external awareness skills. I explained that I didn't have long and needed to leave the office on time, as I was due to go to the cinema that night with my partner. The boss was in the room

Fig.12

speaking to somebody else and I was making my way towards the door. When the boss spoke to me, I had just opened the door to leave. I turned round to face him and explained that I didn't have long. I needed to leave shortly, as I had booked tickets for the cinema. This didn't seem to register with him. He was known as someone who was, shall we say, never short of a word to say. He carried on talking and talking and I was more aware that time was marching on. I remembered the body language training course that I had attended and used some techniques that I had learned. I pointed one of my feet to the door. This had little effect, and he was oblivious to the change in body position. I made this this more obvious and rotated my torso at ninety degrees to him, with both feet pointing to the door. Still, he did not pick up on my desire and need to leave the room. I then made it really obvious. I had my body halfway outside the door with my head turned back to speak to him. Still, he was unaware of this nonverbal communication. I finally gave up. I then bluntly said that I really needed to go and that I would see him tomorrow. I still chuckle about this to this day. You can't win them all!

This experience is important as it shows just how low some people's external awareness is. When someone displays this type of foot pointing, it is a good idea to let the person go. Acknowledging this and mentioning that you detect that it is not a good time and suggest catching up at another time will often result in relief in the face of the other person.

Ready steady go

Fig.13   Fig.14

People who are seated and wish to indicate that the meeting is over will often display the following signals. Weight is shifted to the edge of the seat. (Fig.13) Hands are placed on the knees and

Fig.15

the feet are placed together. Weight is transferred forward to the balls of the feet and leaning forward takes place. Sometimes one foot is placed behind the other. (Fig.14) If standing we may see a weight change as people move to the starter' position. (Fig.15) Be aware if you see these signals. It means that the person wishes to end the engagement. This is a sure sign that the person wants to leave, and quickly. Terminate any meeting quickly if you see this, as they are unlikely to be listening.

Policeman's feet

Fig.16

When people want to create a position of power and authority, they will increase the gap between their feet and the stance will widen. (Fig.16) Policemen and the military adopt this position and those wishing to convey power and authority. If somebody widens their stance, this can indicate being unhappy about something and wishing to take control or affirm their position. If adopting this position, simply narrowing the stance can reduce any tension during an encounter.

Flirtatious feet

Fig.17

When there is a high level of rapport, attraction, or in a romantic environment, the feet will tend to mirror the other person. If a woman feels comfortable in the company of another man and she has crossed her legs, she often allows her shoe to dangle and to bounce up and down. (Fig.17) The toes often hold the shoe. This behaviour is a sign of comfort and quickly disappears if she is uncomfortable with her companion or the environment.

LEGS

The legs also convey clues. They will become more active when excited, in a similar manner to the feet. When observing the legs, we can gain a lot of information from a person's walk. If you are feeling confident or have just received good news, then the pace is quicker. You may have heard the expression "walked with a spring in his step." Think about when you are walking somewhere that you don't wish to go to or are not in the best frame of mind. You may have heard the expression "dragging her feet." Children and teenagers often express displeasure through their legs and feet.

We can pay attention to which part of the body is leading when walking. People who are more cerebral or academic often lead with their head first. Think of an image of an old professor or the eccentric scientist walking with their head leaning forward.

Some people tend to walk with their chest first. These often are more heart centric and emotions are more important in their decision making.

There is the final category and this is prevalent amongst young males. These are people who lead with the groin. A swagger often accompanies this. This shows where their thinking is coming from and doesn't require any further explanation.

Walking types

We can also observe the type of walk that we see. What is the pace like? Are there small steps or large strides? Is it reserved and conservative or do we see a swagger? Is it purposeful or dithering?

Crossed legs

Fig.18

The legs when crossed can indicate both comfort and discomfort depending on the scenario. Often, people, when sitting down, will cross their legs. If sitting down on a sofa, their legs will point at the person they like the most. (Fig.18) The reverse is the case if they don't get on or are not in rapport.

Comfortable legs

Fig.19

When sitting down and feeling comfortable, the legs often are outstretched and we see a crossing of the legs. This is often accompanied by leaning back and taking up more space. (Fig.19) When someone is standing comfortably, their legs will remain relatively static and in a well-balanced position. They will move if they feel excited. The legs give away a lot more information about how comfortable someone is. Let's look at three leg positions that commonly occur when people are speaking in public.

ROCKERS, CROSSERS AND SHIFTERS

Rockers

Rockers are people who rock back and forward on their feet. Often they have one foot in front of the other and rock from the heel to the toe. (Fig.20) While this is less unsightly than the crossing position, it causes a distraction. It conveys nervousness and a lack of confidence as the person moves back and forward.

Fig.20

Crossers

Crossers are people who, when standing up, cross their legs while they are speaking. (Fig.21) This gives them a barrier but looks unsightly to those in the audience. It does not convey an air of authority or confidence. I remember working with a woman years ago who was tall. When she was asked to stand up and present, she had an unfortunate habit of standing, crossing her legs and bending down from the waist

Fig.21

periodically to one side. The message it conveyed was one of a lack of confidence and lack of control. It also looked peculiar. Crossers, when nervous or when lacking confidence, will often have their hands crossed in front of the groin area. It is as if they are trying to make themselves smaller. This is a characteristic of introverted and nervous people.

A shifter

Fig.22

A shifter is somebody who shifts their weight from one foot to the other. (Fig.22) They often bend at the waist from side to side as they do so. I once attended a presentation where the speaker was convinced that he was an excellent presenter. In fairness, his delivery was reasonable. However, he had an unfortunate habit of being a shifter. He also combined this with putting one of his hands in his pockets and engaging in excessive hand movement, which was very distracting! Shifting can be more subtle and uneven weight distribution does not look professional or convincing.

The Glasgow wiggle

Fig.23

Excessive lower body movement can indicate nervousness. It can also convey being untrustworthy. I refer to this excessive lower body movement as the *"Glasgow Wiggle."* (Fig.23) I named this after observing an individual from my home city of Glasgow in Scotland. This individual, despite having "all the chat" and expressive upper body language, had unfortunate excessive lower body movement which conveyed insincerity. It almost looked like there was something uncomfortable crawling in his trousers (or pants for US readers). Remember the expression shifty, it doesn't just apply to the eyes. Once aware of this, I noticed some other people display this. So much so, that satirical comedy shows in Scotland have parodied this with some Scottish football (soccer) managers. People from the city of Glasgow in Scotland may identify with this.

Where to learn?

One of the best places to observe and interpret leg movement is by watching someone on a stage, or someone presenting to a group. In this environment, people will naturally be under pressure and signals will leak. If you want to assess how confident a speaker is, look at their legs and feet. As the feet and the legs are the most honest part of the body, they can sometimes convey some unusual behaviour.

Interlocking behaviour

Fig.24

During periods of stress, the legs and feet sometimes lock. Interlocking ankles and legs can be a sign of discomfort or stress. (Fig.24) Interlocking ankles can occur when the legs are fully stretched and when someone is sitting in a chair. In males, we often see the knees apart and the ankles lock. (Fig.25) Sometimes people will lean forward and have their ankles crossed beneath them. This often

Fig.25

occurs in meetings or when presenting an idea. I first came across this pattern of body language by observing it in myself when speaking to customers and clients. I noticed my ankles were crossing as I sat in the chair when presenting. When I analysed this behaviour and the emotion that I was feeling, it conveyed one of trying to hold something back and of frustration. Now I make sure that when I am in a meeting, if I detect this pattern of behaviour occurring, I unlock my ankles and there is a corresponding shift in feelings as I do so. I recently watched some video footage of a body language expert being interviewed and noticed the interlocking ankles. The upper body, hands and face conveyed one message while the lower legs conveyed

Fig.26

another. This just goes to show how difficult it is to disguise feet and leg unconscious behaviour, even by those in the know. This is very useful information for us. Taking gestures in isolation can sometimes be misleading. If looking at leg and ankle crossing, it is worth paying attention to the amount of tension that somebody is displaying. If they have their legs tightly crossed or their ankles pressing hard against each other, the chances are they're feeling defensive and slightly stressed. (Fig.26)The language always gives us a clue. We talk about someone opening up. You may

Fig.27

have heard people say I just wish that "she would open up," or "he is a closed book."This occurs with the body, too. We describe people as being very closed and not being able to get information from them. We will look at how we can change this behaviour later in the book when we look at how we can use body language to influence people. The second type of interlocking behaviour to be aware of is that of the foot lock. This is more prevalent in females. We see this when someone is seated (Fig.26). The foot pressed into the back of the lower leg. There is a standing equivalent. (Fig.27) It can indicate being shy or being timid. It may also indicate awkwardness.

CHAPTER 6

Shouldering the Torso

I n this section, we are going to look at the clues that we can get from observing the torso and the shoulders. These can give away subtle but important signals.

Torso

When observing the torso, we will draw on the principle that people move towards things that they like, and they move away

Fig.28

from things that they don't. If someone does not like someone the head and torso may move back together. (Fig.28) Think about two people who don't like each other. In a social situation, they will avoid each other and keep as much space between each other as possible. In a business environment, conference or meeting, observe people who dislike each other. Notice how far apart they are. The language helps us out again, "This town ain't big enough for the

Fig.29

both of us!" Conversely, those people who like each other and get on well will often sit together and will lean in. (Fig.29) This can be seen amongst young children who will often fight to sit next to their friend. The language again gives us a clue. When people are getting on well, they talk about being "very close." When things are not going so well, they talk about "drifting apart."

Fig.30

People turn away from things that they don't like. You may have heard the expression "the cold shoulder." We see this when someone turns their body away at an angle from someone they dislike or feel uncomfortable with. Turning the back completely is an extreme example of this. (Fig.30) You may have heard someone annoyed say "He turned his back on me!" When feeling comfortable, we expose our torso. When uncomfortable we try and hide it.

Barriers to entry

Fig.31

Fig.32

We like to protect our torso from any perceived threat. This is where the key organs of the body are located. We will often use barriers to give us greater comfort. Crossing the arms is one such form of a barrier.

Barriers can come in different formats. Many people, when they are engaged in public speaking or have to deliver a presentation, feel far more comfortable behind a lectern. For others, simply holding a book or a notepad in front of them acts as a barrier. Women tend to protect their torsos more than men. This can be seen with the folding of the arms just beneath the breasts. We may see a woman with a book, folder, magazine, or bag in front of them. (Fig.31) Often we will see a display where a woman will have one arm crossed over her abdomen and grab the other arm with her hand. (Fig.32) Rather than adopting a full arm cross, which can show being nervous or fearful, women will often use a subtler version of the frontal arm grab. This is often seen in gatherings with people lacking in confidence or being a stranger to the group. Men have barriers too and often

Fig.33

use a partial arm barrier. This is the "front self-hand" hold. We see this with women, too. We see this position when people are waiting to be introduced by someone to a gathering. (Fig.33) We also see this position when feeling dejected or being scolded. There is usually an accompanying slight bowing of the head too. Men can display additional behaviours in addition to arm crossing. We may see reaching across to fiddle with their watch or perhaps adjusting their cufflinks. These gestures can indicate a moment of insecurity. Sometimes we may see a buttoning and unbuttoning of the jacket. We often see these displays when people are nervous, such as in a dentist's waiting room or a client's office before a big sales presentation.

Hands behind the back

Fig. 34

Compare this to the ultra-confident pose, where the chest is fully exposed and the hands are holding each other behind the back. (Fig.34) As there is a link between the mind-body connection, simply adopting the "hands behind the back" posture and widening our stance will help change our mental state. Sometimes we may witness the "behind the back gripping gesture." The behind the back, gripping gesture communicates a different emotion to the frontal handhold. When the wrist or arm is grabbed, we associate it with self-control and frustration. (Fig.35) One hand grips the other wrist or arm tightly behind the back.

Fig.35

Fig.36

The higher in the arm that the gripping takes place, then the more frustrated or angry the person is likely to be. (Fig.36) This gesture ties in with the language and the expression, "Get a grip of yourself."

Coffee barrier cup

Let's look at one last example with the coffee barrier cup position. (Fig.37) We can see the torso barriers in everyday situations. Rather than cover every single situation, the act of sharpening your awareness will assist you greatly.

Fig.37

Shouldering it

The shoulders can convey lots of useful information, both with position and movement. Someone with rounded shoulders, or who is stooping, will find it harder to gain the respect and command of people that they come into contact with. Compare this to someone with the shoulders back. Think about the typical posture that somebody adopts when they're feeling less confident, depressed or down. The shoulders tend to droop. It is no surprise that when the military is on parade everyone stands with their shoulders back.

Shoulder shrug

Fig.38   Fig. 39

The shoulder shrug is a universal gesture to convey that we don't know about something when asked. It can also mean "What does it matter?" It consists of raising both shoulders in a slightly hunched position. (Fig.38) This is often accompanied by having exposed palms, raised eyebrows and the mouth in a horseshoe position.

The shoulder shrug, when performed unconsciously, is an unconscious leakage. It is different to that performed consciously. When somebody says something that we disagree

Fig.40

with, leakage can occur. The movement is performed unconsciously and not in its entirety. When looking at the shoulders, we may see that only one shoulder moves up slightly. (Fig.39) There may be a subtle display of the palms and the lower lip may turn up slightly. The shoulders can display a lack of confidence. When people are confident, want to make themselves known. The body language is bigger. The head is held higher and the shoulders are pushed back. Conversely, when people lack confidence or are nervous, they literally want to make themselves smaller. We can observe this with the turtleneck effect where both shoulders rise to hide the head. (Fig.40)

The lint picker

Fig.41

Fig.42

If someone picks imaginary pieces of lint from their clothing, often from the shoulder area (Fig.41) or sleeves (Fig.42) of their clothes, this can show that they disapprove, dislike, or disagree with what you are saying.

CHAPTER 7

Armed & Handy

The arms and hands convey a lot of information and clues to those with a sharp eye. They are physically closer to the head. Being closer makes them much more visible to us. People often exert more control over their hands and arms to disguise what they are thinking.

Fig.43

Hand and arm movement can convey a lot of information to us. This can be from general information to more specific clues. Children are often very insightful to look at and observe. They have not yet learned how to mask their intentions and you see body language, particularly with the arms and hands, on full display. People who are extroverts and more confident make themselves bigger. (Fig.43) As the inner thought is reflected in the external expression, we can see this with the arms and hands helping to make somebody appear bigger and occupy more space.

Fig.44   Fig.45

People who feel nervous, or who are introverted, often want to appear psychologically invisible. This is done by using the arms and hands to make themselves smaller. (Fig.44 and Fig.45)

The hand and arm activity can also demonstrate the amount of excitement, nervousness, or calmness that somebody is feeling. We can draw on the principles that we identified when looking at feet and leg movement. When people are feeling positive about things and they're more confident, we tend to see an upward gravity-defying action of the hands and arms. Conversely, when people are feeling negative and less excited, we see the hands and arms in a more static position.

GIVE US A HAND

There are more nerve connections between the hands and the brain than between any other part of the body. This means that the hand positions and gestures that we adopt with our hands give powerful insights into our emotional state. The hands can give away a lot of clues. If somebody is right-handed they will often emphasise the strong points of their argument with their right hand. The reverse is true for left-handers.

Finger-pointing

Many of us have had the experience of somebody pointing at us. It is not a pleasant experience. (Fig.46) Many people do this and

Fig.46

are unaware of it. I recently witnessed this and was done by somebody who is involved in communication training. They were blissfully unaware that they were pointing at the audience. Think about it. What do you do if you are angry with somebody or with a child? There is often a pointing gesture. We often

associate this with a command, "I'm telling you to do it!"

People don't like being told what to do. One of the key principles in the author's earlier work <u>"Inside the Mind of Sales,"</u> is that people resist what you tell them and accept what they conclude. People will generally resist being told what to do unless the person is of sufficient expertise or authority. When authority is used people's critical thinking tends to be suppressed and they will go along with it. This is why so many television stations bring on an expert.

Next time you are watching two politicians, of differing opinions, getting involved in a heated debate, watch out for the finger point. I learned early in my career to avoid pointing at clients or customers. When I am coaching people and I observe this gesture, it is one of the first things that I will advise them to drop. This is relevant when speaking on a one to one or when presenting to a group of people. If you are involved in any profession that involves developing rapport and empathy, perhaps in coaching, therapy, healthcare or a sales situation, I would strongly avoid using any finger-pointing gestures.

Back of the hand point

The back of the hand point involves pointing at people or the audience with the back of your hand. This is often used by public speakers and presenters. While this is not as intrusive as pointing at somebody, it still doesn't feel totally comfortable. It is almost like a swatting action. However, the back of the hand point has its uses. If you are presenting to a large group of people and wish to identify a group of people within that group, then this can be useful. For example, a trainer may say to a group of people that have been assigned into smaller groups, "What does the group over here think?" I try to avoid all forms of pointing and would rather use palm gestures, which we will discuss shortly.

The upward point and chop

Fig.47

The upward point occurs either with one finger pointing up at an angle, but it can also take place with five fingers pointing. (Fig.47) This is usually to the side of the person speaking. Often it takes place as an isolated or series of chopping actions. This action is a reflection of inner thought and the content is literally being chopped. The action is often associated with I

66

agree with some of what you said, however, I don't agree with all of it. The other type of meaning associated would be that there is a *"but"* to what is being heard.

Palming it

Fig.48

Palm display, or lack of it, is a very useful hand display that can give us some clues. (Fig.48) The easiest way to read body language is to think about a situation in the past and notice how it made you feel. The display of palms is associated with a sign of openness, honesty, and conveys trust. Think about somebody accused of something. If they are completely innocent and they're trying to persuade us of this, we often see an opening of the palms and an extension of the arms outwards. Remember that the outer expression reflects the inner thought. They are literally opening themselves up. A word of caution. Some salespeople are aware of this and will overuse palm gestures. This comes across as being manipulative. The display should be natural and not excessive.

I would encourage the use of open palm displays, particularly if you are involved in any profession where you need to convey openness, honesty and trustworthiness. If you are involved in any coaching, therapy, healthcare, counselling, sales or management, I would strongly advise you to adopt this gesture.

Nervous hands

Fig.49

When nervous, we will often see fidgeting and playing with the fingers. (Fig.49) Another sign of nervousness is the hands being slightly damp and cold. This can indicate that the sympathetic nervous system (Chapter 4) is overstimulated, and the person is in a state of fight or flight. A further sign of nervousness is self-hand holding. The language can give us a clue. You may have heard people say, "Can I give you a hand?" Self-hand holding it's very prevalent when people are standing up and are nervous. You will often see this displayed by people who are not confident or nervous when speaking in front of a group. I remember once I was asked to help some people with a pitch that they were doing. As soon as the group stood at the front, they all showed "the standing leg cross" and they were front self-hand holding (Chapter 6). It looked like a choreographed routine! It did not matter what the content was that they were going to be talking about. They did not look confident or believable.

Excited hands

Fig.50

Rubbing the palms together indicates excitement. Think about what happens when you are excited. Your body will move more and the movement is faster. The same thing happens with hand rubbing. (Fig.50)

You may have seen people rubbing their hands together. The speed at which a person rubs their palms together signals intent. Excitement usually consists of rubbing both hands, with the fingers being fully extended, in a fast, vigorous up and down motion. The language again gives us a clue. "He was rubbing his hands with glee." This gesture shows excitement or when something has gone our way financially. It could mean that we have just closed a big deal or have just discovered a way to make some money. I have often jumped up while watching Scotland playing rugby (a game similar to American football) and started rubbing my hands furiously when Scotland has scored a try (or touch down for US readers) with excitement.

Fig.51

If we see a slower pace of rub, often with pulling at the thumb, then the person is signifying that the deal is in their interest more than yours. Be careful when using this gesture in front of people. They can often interpret that you are making money at their expense. (Fig.51)

69

We should differentiate this from "hand washing," which is where the hands are rubbed together as if washing them. Hand washing is a comforting gesture and one that my late father was fond of.

Confident hands

Unless using purposeful gestures to communicate, such as talking with your hands, in everyday activities, the quieter the hands are, then the more control that is displayed. Regulating hand movement to emphasise power has more effect than having arms and hands that fly around.

The finger steeple is a display sign of confidence. The fingers are extended and both hands are pressed together. There are three main positions of the steeple. Fingers pointed up, fingers ahead of you and fingers down. Let's look at these in more detail.

Lawyer's steeple

Fig.52   Fig.53

Let's start first with the fingers up position. (Fig.52) I call this the lawyer's steeple. You will often see this when someone is in a seated position. It conveys a sign of superiority, confidence and superior knowledge. We often associate this position with lawyers who know a legal language that very few of us understand. This is not to be confused with the clenched steeple which can show discomfort. (Fig.53) The degree of clenching reflects the degree of discomfort. This can be observed by noticing the tension in the fingers.

Level steeple

Fig.54

The level steeple is often adopted by public speakers. (Fig.54) It is difficult to perform an upward steeple when presenting and it may appear awkward. Many public speaking trainers encourage people, particularly those who struggle to know what to do with their hands, to adopt either a level or lower steeple position. My opinion is that it is perfectly fine to adopt this position periodically while speaking. However, to have the fingers locked in this position permanently while speaking looks unnatural to me.

Lower steeple

Fig.55

The lower steeple is similar to the level steeple, but with the fingers pointing down to the floor. (Fig.55) Many public speakers adopt this gesture. Women tend to adopt this gesture more. We will look at how we can use steepling to our advantage later in the book. Lower steepling can occur while people are seated too. If seated at a table, then this may be out of sight. It is still an indication of confidence, but not to the same degree as a raised steeple.

HANDSHAKE SECRETS

We acknowledge the handshake in the western world as a sign of friendship. I first came across different handshakes when at a body language training day back in the 1990s. I found that this is a useful part of nonverbal communication to be aware of. The handshake can help gain insight into a particular person. There are different types of handshakes and we will cover these below. The easiest way to think about analysing different handshakes is to think about different people that you have encountered over the years.

Dominant handshake

Fig.56

The dominant handshake consists of having the arm fully extended and thrust out in front of the person. The knuckles are facing up and the palm is facing down. (Fig.56) The torso will often be at an angle. There is a friend of mine who uses this type of handshake and is unaware of the impression that it gives. However, it reflects his personality of being dominant and wanting to be in control. We can sometimes observe this as a finger grab.

Welcoming handshake

Fig. 57

The welcoming handshake involves having the palms facing up and fingers outstretched. A person in authority wanting to reassure and welcome somebody of lower status often uses this. (Fig.57)

Submissive handshake

Fig.58

The submissive handshake involves having the palm up but the fingers closer together and sometimes involves the hand being at a slight angle. This is often used by people who are lacking confidence or feel submissive but can be used by dominant people wanting to reassure someone. (Fig.58)

The double hander

Fig.59

This handshake involves using both hands to greet somebody. Politicians often use it to appear more genuine. (Fig.59) Used with a stranger, it can have the opposite effect. In its genuine form, you will often see this between people who know each other and who are genuinely pleased to see each other.

The elbow and shoulder grab

Fig. 60

Fig. 61

The elbow grab is an attempt to appear even more sincere. (Fig.60) We can observe this among people who know each other well. We can also use it as a way to convey sincerity. An extension of this is the shoulder grab. (Fig.61) If somebody really wanted you to come and join their firm, you may see the "job offer" handshake. The hand is extended out and grabs the shoulder. "Welcome aboard!"

Getting to grips

The pressure we feel in our hands and fingers when shaking hands with another person gives us more clues. A dominant, confident person usually has a firm handshake. Less confident people have a softer handshake. I know somebody who is very dominant and who has a softer handshake. However, his other nonverbal communication conveys very strongly that he is a dominant figure. Sometimes if somebody has injured their hand in the past, or if they are a musician, they may be protective of their hands.

Dead fish

One type of handshake to avoid is the dead fish handshake. This is where the pressure is so weak that it feels like you are shaking hands with a dead fish.

Business handshake

Fig.62

In business, the correct business handshake is to have the hand at right angles to the floor. (Fig.62) We extend the hand out in front of us with the palm on the left-hand side and the knuckles on the right-hand side. The grip should be firm, but not that of a gorilla! Accepted business etiquette is a firm handshake that moves up and down up to three times. Be sure to face someone when you are doing this. Many people are unaware of a proper handshake and the effect that it has on people. It is worth practising this until it becomes unconscious.

Confident hands

Fig.63

Exposing the hands is a sign of confidence and hiding them conveys the opposite. I remember once, when at a public speaking club, somebody was asked to come up and do an impromptu speech. The young man came to the front of the assembled group and stood there with his hands by his side. The moment that he learned about the topic that he had to speak about, his hands immediately shot into his back pockets. (Fig.63). It is important that if we want to appear confident that we are congruent with our body language.

THUMBS

Fig.64

Another nonverbal hand display to be aware of is the thumb display. Displaying the thumbs shows confidence. Lawyers will often display thumbs in court. (Fig.64) When we see thumbs displayed pointing upwards while the arms are crossed, this can indicate someone who is cocky. (Fig.65)

Fig.65

Fig.66

Hiding the thumbs shows a lack of confidence. (Fig.66) At the same public speaking meeting mentioned earlier, another young man was invited up to give an impromptu speech. On learning about his particular topic, he put his thumbs into his side pockets leaving the rest of his hands outside.

ARMS

Arm Crossing

Fig.67

Many people have oversimplified that arm crossing means being defensive. However, it can be a comfortable position for some people. We rarely do this when we are in our own house, though. For some, they cross their arms when speaking when they become aware of their arms and don't quite know what to do with them. (Fig.67) Often when seated, many people will cross their arms. I have heard some say that people cross their arms because they are cold. I don't think this is true unless the temperature is very low. Interpreting the meaning of the "arm cross" requires some more acute observation. We are looking to identify somebody's normal behaviour, a benchmark if you like. Imagine that we see someone who is sitting normally with their arms by their side. We then say something and they cross their arms and lean back. If standing, we

Fig.68

may see a sudden crossing of the arms. This may indicate disagreement with something that you have said. If someone crosses their arms and grabs their arms tightly, this can indicate discomfort. The degree of gripping reflects the amount of anxiety or discomfort. We may also observe the hiding of the hands by making a fist. (Fig.68) This is rarely a good sign and usually shows some discomfort.

Tension spreads

If someone is crossing their arms in frustration or anger, then this will be reflected in outward tension. When crossing their arms, you may see their hands gripping their arms more tensely. You may notice that their hands appear slightly paler. This results from an overstimulation of the sympathetic nervous system. This is indicative of stress or discomfort. Other things to look for are whether the person is frowning, or looking down. Also, observe how tense are the person's face muscles?

Feeling confident

Fig. 69

When athletes win a race, the arms become outstretched and the hands are raised above their head in a victory position. This would be an unusual position to adopt in a normal conversation, but the principle is important to be aware of. The gravity-defying, up/down, position again applies to the arms and the hands. Think about a child who is being scolded. Their arms dropped to the side and are static. When seated, a sign of confidence and superiority is seen when the hands are outstretched and put behind the head. (Fig.69) The legs are outstretched or crossed with the ankle of one foot resting on the thigh of the other leg. Sometimes, the feet are placed on the desk.

Dominance

When we are feeling confident, we make ourselves bigger as we command more space. When people speak, they increase their surrounding space using their arms. We see this with the legs taking up more space too. (Fig.70)

Fig.70

Dominant arms

Hands-on hips is a sign of dominance, authority, and a territorial claim. It can be used as a power signal. (Fig.71) Men use this more than women. Military personnel and police officers often adopt this position when speaking to each other. A widening of the stance often accompanies this. Women, if doing this, do this differently as shown. (Fig.72)

Fig.71

Fig.72

Boardroom dominance

A dominant position that illustrates being in charge and being in control is seen when the fingers are splayed and the body leans forward into the table. (73) We see this in the boardroom or when someone is running a meeting.

Fig.73

Feeling energetic

When people are feeling energetic or excited, we witness a more exaggerated form of movement. You may have heard the expression that someone "talks with their hands." Many excellent communicators, public speakers and presenters are aware of the power of using their hands to emphasise particular points. They know that if they want to convey high energy, enthusiasm and really link into the emotional part of the brain, then using hand and arm movement is an effective way to do this. An advanced technique that many communicators, including hypnotists, use is called "analogue marking." Key messages are reinforced by some form of hand or arm movement. We will look at this later.

CHAPTER 8

Head & Neck

A lot of nonverbal communication takes place in the head area. Many people have learned to control more of the obvious signs, but we can still get a lot of information through careful observation.

Head movement

Let's start with some basics. In many parts of the world, a head nod indicates yes and agreement. The converse to this is the shaking of the head to mean disagreement. There are some countries, however, such as Bulgaria, where shaking the head means yes! To make sure someone is congruent watch for head movement. Some people when agreeing verbally, will shake their heads to the left and right. They are showing nonverbally that they don't agree. Their body language contradicts the words. This is not a sign to accuse somebody of lying. However, it is a clue that the person may not be telling the truth.

Listening head

Fig.74

Another head movement that is useful to be aware of is when the head tilts slightly to one side at an angle. We often observe this in meetings. (Fig.74) It is indicative that somebody is listening and is interested in what you are saying. I have often observed the change in this head position when presenting in meetings as people become more interested.

Dominant head

Fig.75

People who are dominant or confident will walk with their heads held high and often slightly back. The language again reflects this with expressions such as "She walked with her head held high." If the head is tilted too far back, this may show arrogance. Fig.75

Sneering head

The sneering head is an exaggerated form of the dominant head.

Fig. 76

Here we see that the head is lifted back, and is often accompanied by a narrowing of the eyes. Sometimes there is a sneering look. We may observe this amongst people who wish to convey power or think that they are better than someone else. The language reflects this head movement and we have expressions such as "He looked down on me," or "To turn your nose up at somebody." In the UK, sometimes people will touch under the tip of the nose and lift it up slightly. This shows that somebody is snobby or looks down on other people. (Fig.76)

Victorious head

When people are victorious or have achieved something, the head moves back, and they look up. The principle holds true of the "up position" reflecting positivity and success and an anti-gravity display.

Bored head

Fig.77

When the head interacts with the hands, we can convey other messages. Imagine that we are listening to something boring. We may support our heads. What is happening here is that we are supporting the head in an anti-gravity action. (Fig.77)

Interested head

Fig.78

Sometimes people misinterpret the hand on the face gesture as disinterest or boredom. (Fig.78) The main thing to look for is to see if there is any support for the head that reflects anti-gravity support. This can be subtle. An interested head will have no head support.

Disinterested head

We may see the hand on the side of the face with the finger pointing up and the thumb under the chin. (Fig.79) This could indicate a lack of interest or a disagreement with the content.

Fig.79

Shocked head

In the same way that we move away from things that we don't like, we will also do the same with our head. This can be a much more subtle movement, but it's still observable. The language again gives us a clue. You may have heard the expression "I was taken aback." Think about when somebody receives bad or shocking news, they often will move their head back and in many cases their body too.

Negative head

The negative head ties into the principle that things that go up are positive and things that go down are less than positive. Someone who is feeling depressed will be looking down. (Fig.80) They are accessing feelings and emotions and could be talking to themselves. The language gives us a clue. "I just feel down today." The phrase "Keep your chin up!"

Fig.80

is the reference to lifting your head up to break the chain of thought. There is some evidence to support this.

Angry head

Fig.81

When people are angry and start throwing insults at each other, the head moves back slightly and the chin is raised. Fig.81 There may be other displays of anger such as snarling. When you see two people, particularly males, in a competitive aggressive situation, you may see the heads tilt back. The expression "he completely lost the head," reflects the head being tossed back.

Disapproving head

Fig.82

A more subtle head position to be aware of is when the head is looking down and there is tension displayed in the face and the eyebrows. (Fig.82) This can indicate disapproval. Consider speaking to a young child who has misbehaved. What type of expression and head position do you adopt?

Maybe head

Fig.83

This can be seen by the movement of the head from side to side and it is often accompanied by the open palm gesture as if weighing things up. (Fig.83) The lips are often narrow and they go into a downward pointing half-moon position. The stronger the emotion, then the stronger the gesture.

Respectful head

Bowing is a mark of respect. The language again gives us a clue as to the nonverbal action. The expression, "I bow to your greater judgment," is a display of respect. Bowing also occurs when someone feels honoured, for example, a performer receiving applause after a performance. In a business situation, the boss may recognise the contribution that somebody has made to the business or a project in an open forum. The recipient of this acclamation may exhibit a small bow by way of a nod of the head. In an engagement with someone of higher status or authority, the head will often lower slightly. This is a subtle movement, but it is observable. The reverse is true in that those in control will tilt their head back. Bowing is not so prevalent in western society, except for religious or royal figures. However, bowing occurs routinely in Chinese and Japanese cultures. I also observed it when I was travelling in Thailand. For Westerners, bowing can sometimes feel awkward as they are not used to it. If travelling to countries where bowing is considered an everyday practice, someone would be well advised to learn the etiquette associated with it. Bowing, particularly in business, will gain rapport with other people in that culture much more quickly. Remember, we must meet people at their level of reality, not ours.

Subservience

Generally, height is associated with authority and power. People of lower status will try to make themselves smaller. (Fig.84) Bowing also plays an important status role in an interaction between two or more people. A junior member of a company may want to please the boss and will lower his or her body to appear smaller. Think about some of the more old fashioned shops or stores that you may have been in.

Fig.84

The shopkeeper will bow their head out of respect for their customers. This will often be seen in restaurants as well. "Just as you wish, sir!"

Nervous head

Fingers in the mouth can indicate nerves. It's not always the case, though. Some people have developed a comfort habit of putting their fingers in their mouth. They may bite their nails. Some even bite the skin around their fingers in a rare condition known as dermatophagia. It is important to

Fig.85

establish a baseline. You may have heard people say, "I had no nails left by the end" when they were watching something and they were nervous. Biting the bottom lip can indicate being nervous and not knowing what to say or what to do. (Fig.85) It is associated with people that are are subordinate.

Forgetful head

| Fig.86 | Fig.87 |

Self slapping of the head shows forgetfulness. There is a difference between slapping the forehead or the back of the neck. If it is the front of the head, they are displaying frustration associated with forgetfulness. (Fig.86) Someone is annoyed with themselves. If, however, they slap the back of their lower head, this can indicate irritation. (Fig.87) The language again gives us a clue. Many of us have heard the expression "a pain in the neck." The science backs this up and research by Gerard Nierenberg has found that back of neck rubbers are more negative and critical. Forehead rubbers tend to be more open and easy-going.

THE NECK

We may notice that when someone gets frustrated or annoyed, we may see them scratching their neck. In males, we can see this as collar pulling when wearing a shirt. The phrase "they are a real pain in the neck," can be taken literally. (Fig.88)

Fig.88

Fig.89

We must establish a baseline of normal body language behaviour first. For example, if somebody has a habit of scratching their neck, it doesn't mean that they are displaying signs of discomfort. They may just have an itchy neck and have used new detergent. The female neck displays are different. When a woman experiences stress, she touches the suprasternal notch. (Fig.89) This is the hollow between the Adam's apple and the top of the collarbone. This indicates feeling stressed, insecure, threatened, or fearful. It is a sign of discomfort. We may also observe this as playing with the necklace. Men may alter their ties and will touch their faces more than women. Women touch jewellery, necklaces, the suprasternal notch, hair and clothing when experiencing discomfort.

CHAPTER 9

The Eyes Have It

The eyes have often been described as the windows to the soul. When analysing body language, or nonverbal communication, the eyes can reveal a lot of information about what a person is thinking. They are very useful to observe when watching other people interacting. The eyes can convey a lot of information to us through eye movement when accompanied by other body movements.

When two people meet and make eye contact, they find themselves in an unusual situation. They want to look at each other, yet, they also want to look away. This can result in a series of sometimes complex eye movements. When we meet somebody for the first time, we are literally sizing each other up. We are trying to find out if someone is a friend or foe. We also want to find out if what they are saying is of interest and beneficial to us and if we find them attractive. If you observe, you will see this process taking place. The rules of this glancing behaviour are complicated. If we hold their gaze too long, this can create the wrong impression. If we don't hold it long enough, then equally this can have an adverse effect.

Hypnotists are aware of the power of holding eye contact for a long time. Many have perfected the art of the hypnotic gaze to hypnotise people. Many of us will have had the experience of somebody who holds a gaze just a little bit too long. We will also have experienced the opposite of someone who doesn't hold the gaze long enough and whose eyes are darting about all over the place. If we are attracted to someone, we have this conflict of wanting to look at someone that we find attractive. However, we also have the feeling that we don't want to make this obvious.

Think about a young boy and a young girl who are very shy. They may be attracted to each other, but they spend a lot of time avoiding eye contact. We may observe a lot of looking down at the floor. When they speak, there is often limited eye contact. There are two emotions at play here. There is a conflict between the fear and the attraction that they feel for each other. Often sideways glances will accompany this encounter rather than direct eye to eye contact. As mutual attraction shifts to love, then the fear of rejection and shyness dissipates. The lovers eventually come closer together physically and gaze deeply into each other's eyes, often for long periods. That you can identify with this example and have created a mental picture means you must have been aware of it. This example illustrates that not only do we look at what we like, we also move towards what we like.

An eye for it

Let's have a look at what happens to eye contact when we are dealing with status. You may have come across the expression "eyeballing." We see this when boxers stare at each other at close range before a fight. Holding a gaze is a sign of dominance and the one that looks away can often give away power.

Let's look at an example of the gaze in everyday behaviour. Think about a situation when a boss is displeased with an employee's behaviour or performance. The boss holds eye contact with the employee and confronts them. The employee begins justifying themself. The boss continues to glare at the employee. The employee unable to hold the gaze looks down or away in a sign of submission. The employee is literally "losing face." The converse is allowing people "to save face."

Expressions often reflect the physical aspects of behaviour. In the example above, the boss may say "I'm going to be keeping a close eye on you." Or he may say I am going to be "watching you very carefully" going forward. The language is quite literally telling you what he is going to be doing.

Sideways glances

Holding a gaze a fraction too long can be an indication of finding another person appealing or attractive. If we are in a social gathering we may find somebody appealing. We don't want to display lecherous facial expressions and behaviours, but we may hold someone's gaze a little bit longer.

The converse is also true. If there is somebody that we don't like or find appealing then we try to hide any facial and body expressions that could indicate this. We will look at the person less and less. Phrases are often very true. You may have heard somebody say "I just couldn't bear to even look at him." This translates to looking at him causes me discomfort. Most people want to move away from discomfort towards pleasure. You will notice that if someone does not like you, or like what you are saying, they will look at you less. This becomes more obvious as emotions increase.

Under these moderate conditions, emotions are controlled. We may notice the smiles, for those sharp of eye, are false smiles. (Chapter 10) You may have heard people saying, "She is just so false." This is an unconscious response. People often find it difficult to analyse exactly why somebody is false. They just say there is something about them. We may even see nodding which accompanies the smile as we attempt to appear congruent. Smiles are easier to fake. We have more control and awareness over them than we do our glances. We may not be aware of the change in our glances. However, the time we spend looking at somebody we don't like gradually decreases. The brevity of the gaze gives the game away.

Getting the eye

Rather than looking at the smiling and nodding, watch the eyes for a clue. Eye glancing movements are important and the whites of the eyes make this more obvious. We have the expression "staring into the whites of the eyes." We can sharpen our awareness and see the dancing of the eyes. People will initially look at us. They will then look away. In many cases, they are accessing different parts of their internal reality. This carries on until the conversation is handed back to the original person by way of a gaze. It is the length of time that this returning gaze lasts, that gives clues.

To look for more clues with gaze behaviour, think about the expression, "he looked shifty." This often conveys someone who cannot hold your gaze and has shifty eyes. This comes back to the basic principle of inner thoughts being conveyed in the external expression.

WHERE CAN I LOOK

There are some protocols that we can adopt when knowing where to look. Let's have a look at three different gaze zones. There is the business gaze (Fig.90), the social gaze (Fig.91) and the intimate gaze. (Fig.92)

Many of us will have had the experience where someone has gazed in the wrong area. When they do, it can make us feel uncomfortable. If you want to have some fun, next time you speak to a friend or someone you know well, just stare at a spot a few inches above their head. They will turn around and look behind them and ask what you are looking at.

While nothing is cast in stone, it is advisable to be careful with the gazes. Many men often use intimate gaze far too quickly with unintended consequences.

The three gazes

Fig.90 Business Gaze

Fig.91 Social Gaze

Fig.92 Intimate Gaze

95

Eyes up, eyes down

In amongst the dancing eyes, we can get more information when people are speaking to us or answering a question. Eye movement is known and used in NLP (Neurolinguistic Programming.) The eyes move and reflect someone's thinking strategy. I have used this on many occasions with great success.

See up, feel down

Let's start by keeping things very simple. When people want to recall an image or create an image in their internal world, their eyes will move up. When they are recalling or creating an emotion or speaking to themselves, the eyes will look down. Lastly, when people want to recall or hear a sound, their eyes will move to the side.

The two most useful things to observe are whether somebody's eyes are looking up or whether they are looking down. Are they in visual/image mode or are they in feeling/talking to themselves mode? Learning to sharpen your awareness and notice eye movements will assist you enormously in any communication situation. If you are a therapist, counsellor, coach or work in the medical profession, being able to know when someone is accessing an emotion is powerful. It is also very useful when looking at attraction and seduction. We will look at how you can use this information later in the book in the section on how to use body language to influence others. Remember that human beings are complicated creatures. We are looking for clues that we can stack together to help us understand their world. The principle true enough to be true prevails.

DARTING EYES

Imagined or real?

In most cases, if someone is right-handed they will recall an image from a memory by looking up to the left. If someone is left-handed, the reverse occurs and they will look up to the right. If a right-handed person is creating an internal picture, then they look up to the right. The reverse occurs for left-handed people. (Fig.93)

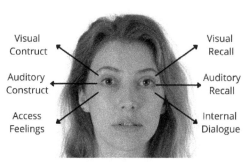

Visual Contruct

Visual Recall

Auditory Construct

Auditory Recall

Access Feelings

Internal Dialogue

Fig.93

I was observing this with my children. My daughter is left-handed and she was fascinated to learn that her eyes moved differently to my eldest son, who is right-handed. My youngest son is also left-handed and his eye movements follow those of a left-hander.

Some commentators have suggested that you can use this understanding of eye movement to spot when somebody is lying. They claim that you can tell whether someone is creating rather than recalling an experience. I disagree with this statement as human communication is very complicated. An understanding of eye movement gives us another clue what is going on in the internal world of somebody and nothing else. It gives us their *strategy* for doing something. That being said, the benefit of noticing and understanding eye movement is that it gives us clues to explore further.

We can use this observation to enhance our understanding of

what people are thinking. If for example, you were to ask somebody who is right-handed, "What did you do last night?" You would expect them to look up to the left. This would indicate retrieving the image of what happened the previous evening. If they looked up to the right-hand side first, this would imply that they were creating an image and therefore making things up.

However, it's not as straightforward as this. Some people access memories first by recalling an emotion or by accessing a sound. In this situation, you may see the eyes move down or to the side.

Second, they may not wish to disclose where they were. They may construct a picture of what would happen if they did first, before accessing the picture of where exactly they were last night.

Eye movement can be very complicated and therefore it is always best to use the Toblerone chocolate or candy bar approach. Like any new skill, it is best to break it down into small bite-size chunks. The first step is to know it is happening. The next step is to notice do the eyes move up or down. Then look and see are they moving to the left or the right. Keep it simple, to begin with. Looking up means seeing a picture, while eyes down means accessing an emotion or self-talk.

I LIKE WHAT I SEE

Let's look now at the pupils. The pupils in the eyes will dilate and constrict in response to external stimuli. They are under the control of the autonomic nervous system and are controlled automatically. We are unable to override their action. Pupils will dilate when we see something that we like or that stimulates us.

This is backed up by the research from Eckhard Hess former head of the department of psychology at the University of

Chicago. The language again helps us out. You may have heard the expression "puppy dog eyes." Pupils also dilate when we see somebody that we like or are attracted to and the expression "bedroom eyes" reflects this. Women's pupils dilate faster than men's.

Ancient Chinese gem traders used to watch for pupil dilation when negotiating prices. Prostitutes, centuries ago, used to put drops from the Belladonna plant which contains atropine into their eyes. This made the pupils dilate to make them appear more attractive. Poker players are aware of the effect of dilating pupils and will wear dark glasses to prevent communicating a good hand. Have a look at the following picture and see which image is the most appealing. Fig.94 or Fig.95

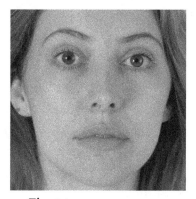 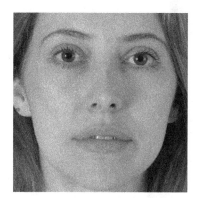

Fig. 94   Fig.95

CHAPTER 10

Mouthy & Nosey

The nose and mouth can give us a lot of information and in this chapter, we are going to explore this.

GETTING LIPPY

Fig.96

The lips are a good indicator of the degree of relaxation and comfort that somebody is experiencing. Those with a sharp eye will notice a difference in the shape of the lower lip. We can use this principle when analysing somebody's nonverbal behaviour. Think about out in the wild when an animal gets annoyed. It snarls and the lips become much thinner and are pulled back. The language again can help out here. You may have heard of the phrase "tight-lipped." You will often see people make their lips disappear and press them close together. We see this with the pursed lips gesture. (Fig.96) It means that you're not keen on something that somebody is saying and that you disagree. The greater the emotion, the greater will be this effect.

When humans become nervous, the lower lip becomes much smaller as it is drawn into the mouth. You may have heard the expression "I had to bite my tongue." Sometimes we see biting of the lower lip, which indicates nervousness or a lack of confidence or discomfort. Those who are sharp of eye may notice the lips being a paler colour than normal when someone is stressed. Conversely, when someone is relaxed, the lips become darker as the balance shifts to the parasympathetic nervous system. (Chapter 1) Hypnotists will look for this as a sign that hypnosis is progressing. This is an advanced observation and comes with practice.

Puckered Lips

When we pucker our lips it means that we are in disagreement with someone or are considering an alternative. Fig.97

Licked lips

Fig.98

Some people lick their lips when they think about delicious food. It is also indicative of somebody evaluating their options. (Fig.98) In an attraction situation, it is done by females as a flirtatious signal to someone that they find attractive. (Chapter 21)

TONGUE DISPLAYS

The tongue is not something that we see often when people communicate. However, there are some displays to be aware of.

Tongue jutting

Fig.99

Tongue jutting can also have different cultural meanings. It can vary from a greeting to rudeness. Here we will look at the more subtle expression. Jutting the tongue out occurs when someone feels they have got away with something, been caught doing something, or have messed up. This action can be brief but can vary in its intensity. (Fig.99) I remember witnessing this a child when a girl had got away with something in class. She stuck her tongue out at me, out of sight of the teacher. She showed that she had got away with it while I was being blamed.

I witnessed this more subtle display with another person who I know well. This person would subtly do this when they knew that they had got away with something. If someone displays this while trying to sell you something and they say that this is the best offer, ask, "Are you sure...?"

SMILING

Smiling is an incredibly powerful gesture. The language gives us a clue, "Smile and the world will smile with you." People have learned the importance of a smile and the need to display it. This has meant that many people learn a fake smile. Have you ever met somebody and while they were smiling, it felt as if they weren't pleased to meet you and it was a fake smile? Your smile must be genuine. Let's look at the difference between a real smile and a fake smile.

Genuine smile

Fig.100

Researchers have discovered that humans have a fake and a real smile. A real smile or "duchenne smile" appears primarily because of the action of two muscles. When these two muscles work together, the corners of the mouth are drawn up and a crinkling around the outer edges of the eyes occurs, causing crow's feet. (Fig.100) These muscles are the *zygomaticus major,* which stretches from the corner of the mouth to the cheekbone, and the *orbicularis oculi,* which surrounds the eye.

It is important to make sure that your smile is genuine and to avoid a false business smile and practice if necessary.

Spotting a fake smile

A fake smile is referred to as a mouth only smile. (Fig.101) With a real smile, we see crinkling of the eyes, lifting and symmetry. This means crinkling of the skin to the side of the eyes, a lifting of the sides of the mouth and a symmetrical smile.

Fig.101

Smiling behaviours

The research shows that women smile more than men. Women will smile for a great variety of reasons and smile regularly to appease men and for no other reason besides habit. It can make a woman appear subordinate or weak in an encounter with unsmiling men. This is something that women should be aware of. This is a generalisation and many of us will have come across stern women who do not smile a lot. The lessons for women are to smile less when dealing with dominant men in business or to reflect the degree to which men smile. If men want to be more persuasive with women, they should consider smiling more in all situations.

Subordinate people smile more in the presence of dominant people in both friendly and unfriendly situations, according to research by Marvin Hecht and Marianne La France from Boston University. We will look in the second part of the book at how we can use smiling to our advantage.

BEING NOSEY

Fig.102

Actions associated with the nose can also give us clues what people are thinking. One of the biggest misnomers when reading body language is interpreting nose scratching as a sign that somebody is lying. (Fig.102) Looking at it in isolation means nothing. We have to establish a baseline. I have found myself frequently having an itchy nose. I will always mention this to the person who I'm engaging with, just in case they misinterpret my communication.

Nose wrinkling

Fig.103

Nose wrinkling is associated with disgust. The mouth will move too, depending on the levels of disgust. (Fig.103) I remember working with one particular individual who used this gesture a lot. It was a sure sign that she didn't agree with things that were being presented. A more subtle version of this is the nostril flare. When we breathe deeply or are emotionally aroused, our nostrils visibly flare. (Fig.104) They may uncontrollably widen in anger when we listen to disagreeable comments made by colleagues around a conference table.

If you see this, the person is not in agreement with you. This is

usually an unconscious response, and I know one individual who does this a lot. While the words convey one meaning, the nostril flare says something else.

Fig.104

CHAPTER 11

Face Blocking Gestures

We can observe covering or blocking signals related to the eyes, ears and mouth. These covering signals are more obvious in younger children. As we grow older, we learn that these are giveaway signs. Consequently, we have learned to control them. As the outer expression is a reflection of the inner thought, signals will be leaked. Desmond Morris discovered that nurses who lied to patients showed a greater frequency of hand-to-face gestures than those who told the truth. When we observe a hand-to-face gesture, it doesn't mean that someone is lying, despite the popular myth. It may indicate that the person could be holding back information or displaying discomfort. It is important to look at other patterns of behaviour and not this in isolation.

EYE BLOCKING

Fig. 105

Let's look first at the eyes. We look at things that we like and look away from things that we don't. Covering of the eyes is an obvious gesture and we see this in young children. As we get older, the signals become more subtle as we learn to cover up. Even as adults, eye blocking occurs. Think about a situation where you have done something that you're not proud of, we may see the fingers cover the eyes just below the brow. (Fig.105) We may also see a shaking of the head. Somebody may think I can't believe that I did that. The stronger the emotion, the more obvious the gesture is.

Fig.106

It can also take place in more subtle ways with one finger pulling at the eye. Fig.106 Sometimes we witness this when someone is sitting down at a table. They may have their hand touching their face in the listening position and their forefinger starts to touch their eye.

Blink and you will miss it

Blinking takes place as an unconscious process but can be consciously overridden. A change in blink rate can a feeling of comfort or discomfort. Some people find it easier than others to identify and spot a change in the blink rate. It is the author's experience that spotting a change in blink rate is hard to do. However, blinking is a powerful nonverbal communication signal. We can learn to use blink rate to our advantage and we will explore this further in Part 2 of the book in the section on how to use body language to influence people. We can however observe eye shutting and we will discuss this next.

Eye shutting

Fig.107

The eyes are constantly blinking and people have different blink rates. When eye blocking occurs we will notice a change in the blink rate. Somebody may momentarily close their eyes rather than blink. (Fig.107) If you speak to somebody and observe this, it can be quite frustrating. If the eyes are tightly closed and screwed up, this can reflect tension and discomfort. This suggests that someone is experiencing something that they don't like. Often this is accompanied by a shaking of the head. On a literal basis, this can mean they don't want to see you're talking about.

Narrowing eyes

We frown and squint at things that we don't like or are suspicious about. You may have heard the expression that her "eyes narrowed." (Fig.108) The eyes narrow and the eyebrows come down. We may witness a frown. This suggests that

Fig.108

someone does not agree or believe what you are saying. The degree of the expression conveys the intensity of the emotion.

EAR BLOCKING

Fig.109

The ears can give clues to what somebody is thinking. Most people cannot move their ears to any extent. Therefore, any observation is going to be confined to touching of the ears. Let's start with an obvious gesture that we have all seen. Think about when you can't hear somebody. The hand is cupped around the ear. (Fig.109) With this action, we are trying to make the ears

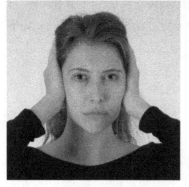

Fig. 110

larger so that we can hear more. The other person will pick up on this. The converse also applies when we want to block out sound and don't want to hear what someone is saying. Think about young children when they don't want to hear something. They will cover both ears with their hands.

Fig.111

(Fig.110) In adulthood, we learn to be more subtle and this can be seen as tugging at the earlobe or playing with the ears. (Fig.111) This can indicate somebody not wanting to hear what you are saying. This is very different to someone is indicating that they can't hear you. We may see rubbing of the ear or even pulling the entire ear forward. This could show that somebody has heard enough or that they wish to speak.

MOUTH BLOCKING

If somebody does not like what you are saying, they will cover up their mouth. Ask a young child if they are lying and immediately, they will cover up their mouth with their hands. (Fig.112) We become more subtle with this as adults. (Fig.113) People's hands will often be drawn to their mouths either when they are speaking or when hearing something that they don't like.

Fig. 112

Fig.113

CHIN TIME

Confident people will have their chin up. For those who are feeling negative, lack confidence or are depressed the chin will be down. The language gives us a clue with the expression "keep your chin up." The chin can convey some important information. Someone who is sitting down and who is supporting their chin with their hand is usually feeling bored or fed up. This ties in with the "gravity down position." This can even take the place of a subtle supporting action with the thumb under the chin. (Chapter 8).

Decision making chin

Fig.114

Fig.115

When people are evaluating something, they will very often stroke their chin. Chin stroking often involves head tilting, looking up or looking down. Sometimes there is a defocusing of the eyes, as people access their internal decision making process. A narrowing of the eyes can also accompany this. When someone tilts their head and is looking up they are seeing pictures of how the suggestion would affect them. There is a slight gender difference here. Males form a triangle between the forefinger and the thumb and stroke the chin in a pulling down motion. (Fig.114)

Females pull away from the chin with the thumb on the underside of the chin and the forefinger on the top. (Fig.115) If a man has a beard, he will often stroke his beard around the chin area as a comforter, rather than when solely evaluating. I once had a beard and found this to be the case.

EYEBROWS

Eyebrow behaviour

Fig.116

Fig.117

Displeasure, frustration and anger is associated with a lowering of the eyebrows in line with the gravity principle. Fig.116 Raising the eyebrows can also add intensity to an expression.

The eyebrows follow the same pattern as the other parts of the body. A raising of the eyebrows is associated with happiness, pleasure and surprise. Raising the eyebrows when looking at somebody increases the expression's intensity, enhances a smile and adds more suggestibility to a pout. The stronger the emotion, the stronger the raise of the eyebrows. (Fig.117) The mere act of raising the eyebrows after asking a question shows somebody that you expect an answer.

Eyebrow flash

Fig. 118

A behaviour that occurs not just in humans but also in chimps is that of the "eyebrow flash." (Fig.118) This occurs when people meet and are pleased to see each other. It is a very quick up and down movement of the eyebrows. If we meet someone and we don't observe an eyebrow flash, this could mean that rapport is not there and that we may not be well received. Japan is a country where the culture dictates that it is not used. Here, it is considered improper or impolite and has definite sexual connotations.

PART TWO

Body Language for Influence

CHAPTER 12

Different Personalities

Recently, I was delivering a talk on advanced communication skills. The subject of body language came up. One of the attendees asked if body language varies between different types of personalities. I thought this was a great question because indeed it does. You can learn a lot about somebody, and their personality type, just by looking at their body language and nonverbal communication. Let's look at some personality types.

PERSONALITY TYPES

Personality types have been around for a long time. Hippocrates called these the four temperaments. He established the four archetypes of people's personalities.

This has evolved. More recently, Myers-Briggs, as an adaptation of the theory of psychological types, produced by Carl Gustav Jung, has produced 16 personality types. This relies on filling in a questionnaire to identify the different types. While this information is useful, it is just not practical to give a questionnaire to someone and then ask them to fill it in. We need a method where we can use our observational and awareness skills instead. This is where our understanding of body language and nonverbal communication will serve us well.

IDENTIFYING A PERSONALITY

My favoured method is the Merrill-Wilson model. It is simple to understand and fast to identify. The four personality types are Dominant, Expressive, Amiable, and Analytical.

There are two main variables to identify a personality type. Are they better with either facts & data or relationships? Are they introverted (low assertion) or extroverted (high assertion)? From this, we get four main types.

Dominant
Fact Based, Extrovert, High Emotional Control.
Analytical
Fact Based, Introvert, High Emotional Control.
Amiable
Relationship Based, Introvert, Low Emotional Control.
Expressive
Relationship Based, Extrovert, Low Emotional Control.

People will move between these boxes in different situations and can be any of the four, but will feel more comfortable in one. The archetype that people fall into is easy to recognise once it is known what to look for. This can be useful when dealing with people. It can give you an indication when communicating and selecting the type of strategy to adopt. I elaborate more on the other signs in the book "Inside the Mind of Sales." In this book, we are going to confine ourselves to what we can observe through nonverbal communication.

The clues

The first step is to identify whether somebody is an introvert or an extrovert. Having done that, then pay attention to the warmth of the greeting that you get. This will give you an indication of whether emotional thinking will influence decisions or not.

Dominant - Aim to be in control

Dominant people exhibit control and power. They often display a firm handshake, direct eye contact and controlled body language with little blinking of the eyes. Expect to see strong eye contact that can sometimes make you feel a little uncomfortable. Dominants will often use the dominant handshake where the knuckles are facing upwards and the palm faces downward. (Chapter 7) The body language reflects control and dominance and they don't move much. When they do move, it is with purpose. They often place the hands on the hips to make themselves bigger. Body positions include standing upright to appear taller with their head back. (Chapter 5) Sometimes they may sit with their hands behind their head in an outstretched position.

These people often like to play power games, which will include having a larger desk or being more elevated than the person with whom they are meeting. To demonstrate control they may swivel the chair to the side or even with their back facing you. This all illustrates the power and control that they perceive they have.

Very early in my sales career, I remember visiting a dominant in his office. He took the whole control aspect a stage further. I was young at the time and was fazed by his behaviour. Not only did he swivel his seat around with his back facing me, but he also did so while eating a bacon roll (a loose equivalent to a bagel if you are from the US.) This was beyond dominance. It was rude, but when I was young, I didn't have the confidence to pull him up on it. At parties, dominants like to make an impressive entrance. They tend not to smile, as this is perceived as a sign of weakness. When they laugh in public, it is in a very controlled way. They very much like other people coming up to them to introduce themselves and to thank them for the invitation. They will be in the centre of the room, surrounded by people of lower status. The people of lower status will exhibit lower status non-verbal signals, such as lowering of the head.

Expressive - Aim to be noticed

An expressive often greets people with a warm greeting and they will display an enthusiastic handshake. They are less formal. They are friendly and warm but are not afraid to say no. They tend to have less control over their body language and as such, it is very expressive. They are animated when they speak. Expect to see palm gestures as they use their arms and hands to communicate their excitement. There is often a higher degree of lower body movement. Expressives move a lot and tend to blink a lot too. Decisions are based on emotion. Expect to see a lot of comfortable eye contact. They are not overbearing and the eye contact moves around a lot. When seated, expressives will often take up a lot of space in some unusual seated positions. As their attention span is very low and they are easily distracted, we often see displays of distraction. Expressives enjoy things that are exciting and new. Expect to see displays of boredom or disinterest if they don't agree with you. They tend to smile a lot and are not afraid to laugh. At parties, expressives are usually the centre of attention and at the hub of what is going on. They like to make a grand entrance acknowledging everyone as they come into the room.

Amiable - Aim to blend in

Amiables are introverts. They aim to please and dislike confrontation and will often see both sides of the argument. They will often greet you with a soft handshake. They are trusting and want everyone to get along. Their body language reflects being introverted, and they tend to make themselves smaller and less conspicuous. They do this by keeping their arms and legs under control and close to the body. They are making themselves less noticeable. Their head is often down in a slightly lowered position to avoid being noticed. Amiables hate confrontation and do not display strong eye contact. They don't like confrontation or being pressurised. Signs of discomfort are often displayed if pressure is applied to them. They move slower and in a more controlled movement. At parties, amiables are often positioned at the side of the room. This ties in with not wishing to be noticed. They are often involved in a conversation outwith groups of people but with other people on a one to one basis. When they smile it is a warm smile and when they laugh it is more controlled. When an amiable enters the room, they aim to do so without being noticed.

Analytical - Aim to work things out

Analyticals love data, details and spreadsheets. They often walk with their head leaning forwards. These people are introverted and very often have very low external awareness. They have very poor eye contact and look down a lot when they speak to you. They have a high degree of emotional control and can give the impression that they are not interested in what somebody else is saying. This comes from their lack of understanding of how to engage. As they have low self-awareness skills, they will sometimes wear some unusual clothes that don't quite fit in with the occasion. Their low awareness skills together with their lack of facial expressions, can come across as indifference. They tend not to smile a lot. This can give the impression of being aloof and unengaged. Fig.119 summarises the distinct personality types.

Changing styles

Using this analysis of body language enables us to adapt our style when engaging with other people. If, for example, we are a therapist and we saw somebody who is an amiable, we would know that we would need to adapt our style. They enjoy reassurance and taking things at a slow pace. Trust is very important to them. If you are dealing with an expressive you would be expected to ask them about their holiday and expect them to talk a lot. They will open with information and will be more than happy to talk enthusiastically and expressively. If you are dealing with a dominant, you would be expected to keep the relationship professional and to get to the point fairly quickly. Dominants like to challenge people. Expect to be challenged and to know everything about your subject. If you are dealing with an analytical, expect to find it difficult to have much of a conversation with them. Everything is based on logic and process. You would be expected to explain what you are doing and to know all the technical details, including all the micro details, if they ask for them. These people do not like generalisation and disorganisation. Expect them to turn up on time. They will expect you to turn up on time, too.

Type	Strengths	Weaknesses
Dominant	Determined Decisive Independent	Lack of Empathy Impatient Domineering
Expressive	Communication Enthusiastic Creative	Disorganised Talkative Unfinished work
Amiable	Diplomatic Supportive Loyal	Not assertive Reactive Change resistant
Analytical	Thorough Disciplined Structured	Rigid Unemotional Perfectionist

Fig.119

CHAPTER 13

Rapport Building

Rapport is a deep level of communication and understanding between two or more people. It is fundamental to any relationship. With rapport, just about anything is possible and without it very little. Before looking at rapport building, let's examine the science behind rapport, beginning with entrainment.

SWINGING PENDULUMS

In 1666, the Dutch physicist, Christian Huygens, discovered that the pendulums of two clocks mounted on the same wall became synchronised to each other. He surmised that the vibrations of air molecules would transmit small amounts of energy from one pendulum to the other and synchronise them to a common frequency.

However, when the pendulums were set on different surfaces, the effect disappeared. The transmitting medium was the vibrating board or wall. After a while, both pendulums would synchronise through the process of entrainment.

Entrainment is a process through which independent systems interact with each other. When two signals are close to each other in frequency, they fall into a single frequency, just like when the pendulums started to swing in synchronisation. The phenomenon also extends to the biological world, where examples include those of synchronising fireflies and in humans with the resetting of the body clocks by sunlight (circadian entrainment). The "entraining" signal can be from inside the body or from outside. Entrainment is an unconscious process and breathing can become entrained with the beat of the music.

Experiments have shown that when individuals interact socially, for example in conversation, the rhythms of their actions become entrained. It is not merely enough being in the same room, there has to be mutual attention for this to occur. This is implying that there is some sort of connection that connects people and the key ingredient is mutual attention to each other.

BUILDING RAPPORT

We can use this principle to build rapport. In simple terms, this means that the more alike you are to somebody else, then the more rapport you will build with them. This doesn't just apply to interests, hobbies and liking the same sports team or type of food. It also applies to nonverbal actions as well. We can see this with young girls who dress similarly or wear the same clothes. This means that in nonverbal communication, the more you show similar nonverbal or body language displays to another person, then the more rapport that you will build with them. This is a very important principle.

People who are in rapport have similar body language and will mirror each other. This is a perfectly natural process. My preferred method when wanting to build rapport with somebody is to develop an intense desire to get to know them and to show a sincere interest in that person. By doing this, my body language automatically synchronises with the person who I'm wanting to engage with.

I recently had an experience while speaking to somebody with whom I get on with and we were speaking in a video conversation. Something interesting happened as soon as we switched our cameras on. After speaking for a minute or two, I notice I had copied this person's body language. My hand was positioned to the side of my head identically to this person. We were mirroring each other!

Before we look at mirroring and matching, let's look at the principle of stacking.

Stacking

The more patterns of nonverbal communication that we display that are like the other person, then the stronger will be the connection. We discussed the principle of stacking in Chapter 1.

MIRRORING & MATCHING

Mirroring and matching means copying. It means displaying the same body language and nonverbal communication as the person with whom you are interacting. There are many ways that we can mirror and match. We can witness mirroring in social situations and by observing people in restaurants, bars and cafes. It's like a dance and occurs at an unconscious level.

Once aware of this, you will notice how people lean towards each other, adopt similar body positions, and then mirror each other. When people first discover and notice mirroring, it is often a major revelation. There are three methods for doing this.

Mirroring

Mirroring is copying somebody's body language just as if looking at ourselves in a mirror. If somebody raises their right hand, then to mirror them, we would raise our left hand. Mirroring is very common in both social and business situations when rapport is present.

Matching

Matching is a form of mirroring which is done as if standing behind someone rather than facing them. When matching someone, if their right hand is raised, then we would raise our right hand. I prefer using mirroring as this occurs naturally and unconsciously, but matching works too.

Cross matching

With cross-matching, the body language is matched not directly but covertly. An example would be if the other person is moving their foot up and down, then we would raise our finger up and down at the same tempo.

A Word of Caution

When people first learn about mirroring and matching, some think that it is manipulative. They think that there is no way that they could do it. They worry and have a fear that they may be caught. This is a perfectly natural reaction. However, mirroring occurs naturally and in everyday life. If you are not convinced of this simply go to a café, sit down and watch people and you will see mirroring taking place.

However, to help get the process started, the best way to practise is in a social situation to satisfy your critical mind that it works. Then, when feeling comfortable with this, incorporate it into any environment.

When I first discovered mirroring, I was sceptical and wondered if it would work. I decided to test it. I remember being in a pub with a client and noticed that we were both leaning against the bar. We were facing each other with our bodies slightly angled towards the bar. I spotted we were both mirroring each other and I decided to test leading. I increased the angle of my body to the bar. To my surprise, the person that I was speaking to, not long afterwards, copied me. Wanting to test this further. I then increased the angle again, and the other person copied me. I was stunned by this. It had worked just exactly as I had been told it would.

Some people, when they discover mirroring and matching, go all out and attempt to copy somebody's every move. This can come across as creepy. We want to be acting naturally and not behaving unusually. We don't want to draw attention to ourselves.

Let's look at two methods to improve mirroring. My favourite method is method one. It is the most powerful and the easiest to incorporate into your everyday communication.

Method 1

The best way to mirror somebody is to have a genuine desire to get to know them. This involves changing your thought process and your outlook. I have found that the best way to do this is to suspend judgement and to develop a curiosity about that person. It has surprised me over the years with my interactions with different people as to just how much knowledge people have and in unusual areas. Getting into a habit of developing a curiosity to learn from someone else is a good habit to get into.

Besides this, looking for something positive that you like about another person is enough to help flip your mind into a more positive state. It could just be down to liking the type of jacket or outfit that they are wearing. For more details on state control, the reader is referred to the author's "Inside the Mind of Sales." This method, in my opinion, is the most powerful as we are linking into the limbic or emotional brain and is done unconsciously.

Method 2

Method two relies on a more conscious approach. This involves consciously changing your body language to match that of the other person. We need to be careful because, as this is a conscious process, it can sometimes come across as quite clunky. The best way to do this, if copying a limb or body action, is to wait for six seconds after somebody has changed their body position and then move into a similar position. Cross-matching can also be used, and this is more covert. While my preferred method is method one, method two has its merits. It is useful where there does not seem to be natural chemistry and the connection does not appear to be happening.

ADVANCED RAPPORT

To influence someone, we first have to have rapport. It is the magic ingredient. With it, just about anything is possible and without it, very little. Once we have rapport, we can look at influencing people.

Pacing and leading

Pacing and leading comes from the world of hypnosis and NLP (neurolinguistic programming) which is software for the mind.

We can use this principle when using nonverbal communication.

Pacing

Pacing means pacing what a person is doing. The more alike that you are to somebody, then the more rapport that we will generate. People like people who are like them. We can reflect back on what someone is doing through pacing. This sets up a biofeedback loop and we can use body mirroring. We can, however, go even deeper and use pacing in other areas of nonverbal communication too.

A very powerful method that we can use is that of matching somebody's blink rate. Blinking takes place largely unconsciously, but the conscious mind can override it. We can take advantage of this and match the blink rate of the other person. This is so subtle and covert that they do not pick it up, and it's very powerful.

Another powerful action that can be used is to mirror somebody's breathing rate. A word of caution here. If you start looking at somebody's chest, particularly if you're speaking to a female, this is likely to break any rapport that you may have developed. An easier way to do this is to watch somebody's shoulders. They will rise when someone breathes in and fall when they breathe out.

An even easier method to detect breathing is being aware that when people speak they breathe out. You can simply mirror the pattern of their breathing, knowing that when they speak, they are breathing out.

Going for a walk

A natural phenomenon that occurs when people are in rapport is that their legs synchronise when walking together. You may have noticed this in the past. We can use this phenomenon when we meet somebody and walk with them. Simply synchronising your legs with theirs as you walk, develops unconscious rapport. Using something simple like this enhances the stacking principle.

I once met a client with whom we weren't naturally on the same wavelength. We were meeting to explore having an external consultant come in to help them. The client suggested we go for a coffee. As we walked to the coffee shop, I wanted to make sure that we were building rapport quickly. Simply matching my legs and synchronising with client created initial rapport and began the stacking process.

After the initial meeting, they invited me back at a later date to meet with the client's boss. At the second meeting, I wanted to build rapport quickly. I got myself into the correct state and enhanced this with some conscious mirroring of the boss' body language. During the meeting, I noticed that not only were the boss and I mirroring each other, but that the other individual was mirroring as well. This meant that I was in rapport with both of them. As the meeting drew to a close, the boss summarised that we all seem to be of like minds.

Leading

Once we have paced, and mirrored somebody for a while, we can change our body position and notice if the other person begins to follow you. If the person begins to follow, we have the phenomenon of leading. Leading is a good indicator that rapport has been built. If we find that when we begin to lead that the person does not follow us, we have not built up enough rapport yet. Simply go back and pacing the person for a longer period.

We can observe pacing and leading when groups of people are standing together. When the dominant person changes body position, the others will often follow. In the next chapter, we are going to look at how we can use body language to get people to like us.

CHAPTER 14

Getting People to Like You

Getting people to like us is another part of stacking. Many people decide whether they like us within the first few seconds. Research has been carried out with people conducting job interviews. They were instructed within the first minute to write down what they thought of the candidate for the job. The after interviewing the candidate for half an hour, they were instructed to write their thoughts down again. What was found was that the interviewers hadn't changed their minds.

The easiest way to think about getting people to like you when using body language is to think about what is it that people who are likeable do? We simply model them and do what they do. Now think about somebody who is disliked. What type of nonverbal actions do they display? We then simply do the opposite?

Nobody likes miserable people. People who are upbeat and who are pleased to see you have body language that reflects this. Think about when a dog is pleased to see you or a young child runs up to greet you. The body language is one of excitement and it is contagious. How good does it feel when this happens and when someone is genuinely pleased to see you?

Let's look at some of the science and how we can use this to assist with getting people to like us. Mirror neurones were discovered by accident by researchers Giacomo Rizzolatti and Vittorio Gallese at the University of Palma in Italy. They were studying activity in monkey brains. They found it did not matter whether an action took place or was observed, it was the same regions of the monkey's brain that were activated. This led to the concept of the mirror neurone. Similar results were observed when looking at the brains of humans. The mirror neurone is a bit of a misnomer. Today, it is generally agreed that there is no such single neuron at work, but a network of neurons working together.

This implies that the more attention that we give to an observation, then the more likely we are to copy the behaviour. We see this when we meet people who have different accents. Our speech and accent change accordingly to enable us to fit in better. This means that the more we imitate other people, then the more we like them and the more they like us.

Dr Ulf Dimberg, from Sweden in 2000, carried out an experiment where he showed volunteers frowning, smiling and with expressionless faces. Even if trying to control our emotions and expressions in every case, minute expressions occurred. This showed that mirroring was the natural tendency.

True meaning

We are always communicating, even when we are attempting not to communicate. It is the meaning attached to the communication that we are giving out that is important, and not the meaning of what we think we are communicating. If a student props her head on her hands while listening to a lecture, she may be interested in the topic, but the message that she is conveying is one of boredom. This body posture is unlikely to do her any favours with the lecturer. It is good to practise getting into the habit of thinking about or becoming more aware of what sort of message it is that you are conveying.

Mind-set

The principle that the outer expression reflects the inner thoughts and having the correct mindset will accelerate this process. The accompanying audio will help with this. If you want someone to be interested in you and to like you, then you have to be interested in them and like them.

The power of the brows

When human beings meet each other, a sign of friendship is shown by raising their eyebrows. This brief up and down action is known as the "eyebrow flash." This has been discussed in Chapter 11. It ties in with the principle that an upward anti-gravity action is a positive action. A gravity gesture and downward action is a less than positive one.

We can use this knowledge of the eyebrow flash to get someone to like us. It is very powerful and can be used both in business and personal situations. I decided to test the efficacy of the eyebrow flash. When my son was younger, I pushed him in his buggy, or stroller, to the nursery or kinder garden most mornings. As I left at a similar time each day, I would often encounter the same people walking in the opposite direction. During the daily walk, I would see the same man and woman walking together in the opposite direction. Every morning they would walk past me with no acknowledgement. This went on for months. I decided one day to use the eyebrow flash. The reaction was instantaneous and astonishing. The man immediately jumped out of his internal world, flashed his eyebrows back at me, nodded and smiled. It was interesting that on every subsequent walk when the man spotted me in the distance, he would immediately flash his eyebrows, nod and smile. I had gained rapport with this man and his wife without saying a word. If you want to get people to like you and know if they genuinely like you, watch for the eyebrow flash.

As human behaviour is complicated it does not work on every occasion because some people are so engaged in their internal world and in trance that they may not even observe you. If they observe you and you don't get an eyebrow flash, then they may not be friendly towards you and some more rapport building may be required.

Smile and the world smiles with you

The second stage in a greeting after the eyebrow flash is the smile. Paul Ekman, when conducting research studying faces that signalled sadness and distress, noticed that he felt terrible afterwards. Ekman and his colleagues monitored the way their bodies changed. They found markers that showed that sad expressions changed their autonomic nervous system. It was as if they were actually feeling sad themselves. This ties into the mirror neurone concept mentioned earlier. When smiling or when we see another person smile, we mentally simulate that action and feel happier. Just the simple act of smiling triggers a rush of positive neurological activity, which lowers stress and uplifts moods. Dopamine increases our feelings of happiness and the release of serotonin reduces stress. On a surface level, we are more prone to reciprocate what we see around ourselves and mirror that internally. Neuroscientist, Marco Iacoboni, explains that when we see people smiling, our "mirror neurons" fire up too. This initiates a flood of neural activity that brings on feelings that we typically associate with a smile. We don't need to infer what someone is feeling. We experience it, just in a milder form.

Being genuine

It is important to display a genuine or "duchenne smile." Any smile that is dead from the nose up is a false smile (Chapter 10). As a recap, a genuine smile is one where we will see a crinkling of the skin around the eyes and the lifting of the corners of the mouth. The language gives us a clue. There is an expression known as the "Pan-Am smile". This expression came from flight attendants who always had to have a smile, even if it was insincere.

To become familiar with what a real smile looks and feels like, get into the habit of practising this in front of the mirror. Notice how there is more tension around your upper cheeks when you smile sincerely. The easiest way to do this is to get into the right state and develop a genuine desire and curiosity to meet that person.

In addition to being a great rapport builder, smiling and humour can act as a diffuser when in tense situations.

Look into my eyes

People like people who look at them and pay attention to what they are saying. Nothing is more annoying than someone who has fleeting eyes while you are speaking to them. This is very evident and can be observed when people are at a gathering where there are lots of people. Many speak to each other while looking around to see if there are other people they should be speaking to.

It is best to confine your gaze to the business gaze in a business environment and the social gaze in a social environment (Chapter 9). If you are a male, be careful when engaging with a female that your eyes are not wandering to the chest area. The wandering eye is generally not appreciated.

When meeting someone and looking into their eyes, pay attention to their pupils. Pupils dilate when we see something that we like. They will constrict when we see something that we don't.

If you feel uncomfortable looking straight into someone's eyes, you can use the hypnotist's trick. Instead of looking straight into the eyes, simply look at a spot in between the eyebrows, above the nose. This will help you maintain the gaze longer if you feel uncomfortable with gazing into someone's eyes.

Getting heady

We have already learned how to interpret head movements. We can now use these principles to show people we like them and, in return, they will like us. A powerful head signal that illustrates that we are listening is the head tilt, which we have already explored. Simply tilt your head to one side slightly at about 30 degrees to show that you are interested. This also plays a part in the language of attraction, which is explored in great detail in Chapter 21.

Nodding

Another powerful head gesture we can use is periodic nodding. This occurs at an unconscious level when people are listening. Most people are unaware that they are nodding. Even someone not trained in body language will unconsciously pick up that you are nodding. This is a subtle nod and is not like a nodding dog toy. It is also important to keep the head level or slightly looking down, as having your head too far back can convey arrogance.

Matching up

We have discussed that the more that you are alike to somebody, then the more that they are going to like you. As we are confining our discussion to nonverbal communication, it helps to make sure we are as alike the other person as possible. We can do this through mirroring, matching and pacing. We have discussed this in the previous chapter. Your clothes, choice of accessories and even matching a choice of drink or food create rapport. It is as if being an extension of someone else.

Arm touching

A light touch on the arm dramatically increases compliance. This applies to several requests including asking for money, to getting a woman's phone number.

Studies show that touching someone on the upper arm, for just a second or two, can affect how helpful they will be. Other studies have shown that the same subtle touch also significantly increases the likelihood that people leave a tip for waiters and waitresses. It also has the effect of increasing participation in supermarket taste tests, causing people to drink more in a bar, and to become involved in charity work.

American researchers in one experiment approached people in the street and asked them for a dime. Touching them briefly on the upper arm increased the likelihood of getting the money by 20 per cent. This also has the effect of increasing the likelihood that people will sign petitions. In nightclubs, women accepted the offer of a dance over 50% of the time after even the briefest of touches on the arm. The doubling of chance also occurred when asking for phone numbers by researchers in the street. It is important to mention that this is a brief touch and not a grab!

CHAPTER 15

Changing Moods

In this chapter, we are going to look at how we can use body language to assist us in enhancing and optimising our mental state. We discovered in previous sections that the outer expression is a reflection of inner thoughts. We also learned that inner thought can be affected by outer expression. If someone is in a bad mood or is angry then there is a body position associated with that. Have you ever seen someone who is angry that is smiling?

We can therefore change our mood by altering our body position. You can experiment with this. Next time you feel depressed, look up and notice how difficult it is to remain depressed. If you are feeling nervous, adopt a stance with your hands behind your back and your feet slightly wider apart. Now look up, and notice how the feelings change. Try steepling your hands upwards when sitting and notice how the feelings change.

In chapter 2 we covered this mind-body connection and referenced the work of Amy Cuddy. Amy discovered and put the science behind what hypnotists and NLP practitioners have known for a long time. Changing posture means that our physiology changes too. This means is that if we change our body position, then our state of mind also changes.

To get the desired mood or state, simply adopt the body position associated with that state. Then revivify or intensify the experience. Try to adopt as many of the positions and layer them. For example, if you wish to appear confident, there is little point in widening the stance, and then looking down with your hands holding each other in front of the crotch and with the shoulders slumped. The easiest way I find to do it is to recall the emotion and the body language follows. However, when learning, you can do this the other way around. Now we are going to take this a stage further. The body language position starts the change, but the real secret is in amplifying the correct emotion. Let's look at how we can do this and remember to be playful.

Find a quiet place where you can be on your own and not disturbed. Stand up and close your eyes. Now think of a time when you were at your very best. You set out to achieve something, you went for it and you succeeded. If you can't think of anything, just pretend. Stand as you were standing and see what you saw. Step into that picture as if experiencing it through your own eyes if you have not already done so. If the picture is stationary, then make it move. If it is in black and white, make it in colour and turn up the colours and the brightness. Now put your hands out in front of you and trace the size of this picture. Now make the picture bigger and as big as an IMAX screen. See what you saw, hear what you heard, smell what you smelt and taste what you tasted. Bring back those feelings. Imagine that there is a dial in front of you that says experience enhancer. Turn that dial to full and notice how you feel. The key to this is to be playful. Don't try to analyse. This is not the part of the brain that we wish to engage. Hold that body position. We can use this mind-body connection together with imagination to tap into the emotional centre of the brain. This is a fast track method for getting into the state that we want to get into in advance for any meeting or encounter.

People are often nervous about situations and often play a mental movie about what could go wrong. You may already have seen this when watching television or in movies. You may see someone who is nervous or apprehensive about either approaching someone of the opposite sex, or speaking to their boss about a pay rise. You may have seen an actor in a movie, or a TV show, or even at the theatre, talk to himself and say, "Come on you can do this!" They give their body a shake, hold their head up and then walk purposely to meet the other person.

The fastest way to change someone is to change yourself. If what you are doing is not working, then try something else. Like any new skill, this requires practise and raising your awareness levels. One of the most powerful things that you can do when using nonverbal communication is to use your state and body language together.

CHAPTER 16

Dress to Impress

There is a phrase, "you never get a second chance to make a first impression." Many people, when they are learning body language, read books and study. However, they fail to realise that it's not just the gestures but how we adorn our body and use other accessories that give out clues.

Remember that the more alike that you are to somebody, then the more rapport that you will build with them. If you are in business, then this means that they are more likely to engage with you if you are alike them. It is the midbrain or emotional centre that drives the decision making process. The critical mind then backs this up with some form of logic. Remember, for something to be perceived as true, it doesn't have to be true, it only has to be perceived as plausible.

When considering what clothes to wear it is worthwhile considering what the people that you will be engaging with are wearing. Clothing should be appropriate to the environment. I don't think that it does any harm to be slightly smarter or slightly overdressed for the occasion. Many people have said that it shouldn't matter what you wear. They say that you shouldn't judge a book by its cover, but book covers do indeed help to sell books.

We do make generalisations. We compare our experience to a previous experience to give us a map of the world. Have you ever been used to dealing with somebody who dresses either in a business suit or a uniform? Then when you see them dressed casually, perhaps wearing shorts and a tee-shirt, somehow it doesn't seem right. They just seem like a different person. How would a judge look dressed in a tee-shirt, shorts and flip-flops? We have seen this with performers on stage. When we see them without their custom costume or makeup, it can change our perception. Clothing can be used to extreme effect as displayed by the vintage rock band KISS.

Let's look at some things to consider when dressing and incorporating accessories. Rather than detailing specific guidance for each sex, it is better to lay down some principles. When selecting a wardrobe, it is worthwhile considering the impression that you want to give. Let's start with shoes.

Footwear

Footwear should be appropriate to the environment and to the people that you're dealing with. Flip-flops may be comfortable, however, would this be appropriate if you want to convey authority? When selecting footwear, it's worth making sure that shoes are clean and polished. If you are dealing with older people, they will be familiar with the expression "judge a man by his shoes." Ex-military will often have very shiny shoes and expect you to have the same. I remember speaking to one individual who is ex-forces and who was looking to hire someone. I had recommended a candidate to him and he immediately picked up on his shoes in the feedback to me.

Remember, we must meet people at their level of reality and not ours.

Business suit

As time has moved on, dress has become more casual and varies from country to country and from city to city. It is worth looking at what your customers or clients are wearing to give you a sign of what is expected. Banking and finance in the City of London demanded conservative dark suits and black shoes for men and was very much part of the uniform. It has relaxed more now. If however you work in marketing or something more creative, wearing a dark pinstripe suit could come across as too formal and stiff. This may indicate lacking imagination for creative people.

Necktie

A necktie is still worn in some industries and some countries. I once worked for a Swiss private bank where it was not permissible to take your tie off while in the office. Neckties communicate a message. Are they discrete and conservative or are they loud and colourful? I remember years ago there was a fashion for novelty ties. Consider if you are wearing a necktie is appropriate for the occasion? You may enjoy novelty ties with flashing lights that make strange noises. However, does this create the right impression for your customer or clients? While these may convey the image of someone fun, if you were visiting a lawyer or a surgeon for a serious matter, you probably wouldn't expect to see Mickey Mouse with a flashing nose on his tie. When working in asset management, I always found it useful to wear a tie, and then take it off whenever the situation dictated.

Shirts and blouses

It never ceases to amaze me that some very highly paid senior people in finance and asset management wear shirts that are frayed and worn at the collar or cuffs. Sometimes, the white shirts had a grey tinge to them. I have visited clients with a fund manager who managed billions of dollars, and yet the clothes did not reflect the responsibility and seniority of managing that amount of money. Remember that we are always communicating not only with our posture or gestures but also with what we are wearing.

Cosmetics

People use accessories and cosmetics to change their appearance and to create or enhance their image. This does not happen by chance. They do this for a reason, usually to create a favourable impression or to stand out. We only have to look at the stage makeup that the veteran rock band KISS have used, to see the profound effect that this can have. Remember, the more alike that you are to somebody then the more rapport we have with them. When women go out in groups for the evening, it is rare to see a glamourous made up woman and an unmade up woman wearing sports gear, make a pair for a night out.

Accessories

Give some consideration to the image that you want to convey to those with whom you are engaging. You may enjoy wearing a skull and crossbones ring on your finger. However, does that convey the right impression to somebody that you are giving legal advice to? Equally, while an expensive set of cufflinks may fit in nicely in finance or asset management, would this work so well if your customers or clients were farmers? They may have the opinion that you look too formal and perhaps stuffy.

Also, pay attention to jewellery. I remember once visiting a client after I had treated myself to a new watch. This client liked expensive watches and cars. He immediately noticed my watch. The conversation then turned to watches. My watch had communicated to him we both had similar interests. I recently spoke with a client who had an interest in fountain pens. Having a similar interest builds rapport. Your accessories and clothing will build rapport with people. You only have to look at people who go to a football or soccer match to see them adopting the same colours, similar shirts and accessories. It is like a uniform or an identity statement.

Hairstyle

Nonverbal communication takes place not just with the clothes that we wear, but with the way we change our appearance. Hairstyles can create an individual look, together with facial hair. They are always giving out clues. It would be unlikely to see a banker with hair flowing down his back and sporting a long goatee beard. However, this would not be out of place for a biker as part of a motorcycle gang. Equally, purple or pink hair would not work well in banking or finance but would be seen more in the creative industries.

When analysing, we don't want to prejudge people. We are merely trying to gain clues and insights. We use these to give us more understanding of that person's map of the world. There are always exceptions and we want something that can help us and that is true enough to be true. There are no hard and fast rules regarding clothing, but remember we are always communicating even if unintentionally.

CHAPTER 17

In Sales

Let's look now at how we can utilise body language in the sales environment. We have already covered how to build rapport using body language and nonverbal communication in Chapter 9. In this chapter, we are going to look at how we can use additional body language and nonverbal communication to help us become more persuasive with the sales process. The reader is invited to refer to the author's work "Inside the Mind of Sales" to learn more about the mind and sales in depth.

We are constantly being bombarded with information, a lot of which is processed unconsciously. We are not aware of much of it. In a sales environment, we want to make sure we get as much information as we can when meeting potential customers. Consider meeting a customer in their office or premises. This is an environment where they feel comfortable. This is their den and they will decorate it accordingly. There are clues everywhere. There may be pictures on the wall, photographs, awards, or trophies. All these will give indications about their family, their interests and any successes that they may have had.

It also gives an insight into their values. A lot of pictures of children and family show a high priority of the family. This gives us an excellent opportunity to ask questions and show a genuine interest. Pictures with famous people can indicate self-importance.

That's my seat

Sometimes, the meeting may not be in the client's office but may be in a meeting room. It is always worthwhile asking where they would like you to sit. People are generally territorial. Many like to sit in the same seat in a restaurant, a bar, or in a meeting. I was speaking to the local lollipop man. A lollipop man or woman is someone with a stick with a circular part on top that they use to stop the traffic. They help the children to cross the road. This man likes his routine. After he has finished his duties, he likes to go to the park and sit on the same bench while he drinks his tea from a flask. We were having a discussion one day and he mentioned he went down to his usual bench and that there somebody else was sitting there. He felt quite put out. Never underestimate the power of territory and assumed territory.

We often find that in meetings, people sit in the same seat. If you arrive at the meeting and take the seat that they normally sit in, this can unconsciously annoy them. Remember, we are trying to stack as many things as we can in our favour, and not the other way around! If a receptionist shows me into a meeting room, I ask the receptionist where I should sit and where does the person who I'm meeting normally sit.

Be careful if you are selling to somebody or are communicating with a client while in their house to make sure that you are not sitting in their normal seat.

Rapport in sales

The easiest way to develop rapport is to have an intense desire and curiosity to find out more about the person who you're speaking to. Something powerful to use is to adopt the same body language and mirror somebody. Remember to allow at least 6 seconds before you change your body position. You can also blink at the same rate as the person that you are speaking to. This will set up an unconscious synchronisation between the two of you. This is rarely picked up in conscious awareness and it's very powerful.

The easiest way to exhibit that you're listening is to do the following. Lean forward slightly. We lean towards things that we like and then tilt your head slightly at approximately 30 degrees to one side, which shows listening. A periodic nod indicates that you are acknowledging and in agreement with what that person is saying. Remember to have a relaxed facial expression. To gain extra rapport frown slightly when someone conveys bad news or troubles that they are experiencing shows empathy. To measure for rapport with a customer or client, watch for unconscious nodding, the tilting of the head and any change in their leaning angle.

Sales presentation

We can use body language in several ways to help make a sales presentation more effective. The first thing to do is to have some form of sales aid or sales brochure with you. Always remember to turn this upside down if you're sitting opposite a client or customer for maximum effect. When you put the sales brochure on the table, this causes the person to lean forward to look at it. Inexperienced salespeople will often hand a brochure to a customer or a client. This is the wrong thing to do. It is human nature to pick up the object, touch it and flick through it. While the customer or client is flicking through the sales aid aimlessly, they are not listening to you. It's also very hard to get it back from them and it would appear rude to snatch it back.

A useful technique is to use a pen as a pointer. When you are presenting and using a pen, the customer or client's eyes will be looking at the pen. To get people to look up simply lift the pen to eye level. This can be made even more efficient by bringing the pen up at an arc rather than in a straight line. Magicians are aware that the eyes follow an arc rather than a straight line. We can use this to our advantage when we bring the pen up.

An even more effective way to use body language to build rapport and get more engagement with a client or customer is to sit on the same side of the table as them. If this is not possible, then sit at 90 degrees to them. I remember when I was the manager for a life insurance company. Besides my desk, there was a circular table. There were no corners and therefore there were no barriers on the circular table. I always had more conciliatory meetings there and saved the main desk when I needed to convey authority.

Asking for the order is where a lot of salespeople go wrong. We need to control certain parts of our body as we observe what is going on. After asking for the order, the first thing that we need to do is to keep our mouth under control. This means, quite simply, shutting up and keeping quiet. There may be excitement, apprehension or nervousness. There is a tendency to babble. This must be resisted at all costs. Positive eye contact must be displayed. The body language should be one of relaxed expectation.

The next thing to look for is the reaction of the other person. There will usually at this point be a change in body language.

We may see some biting or narrowing of the bottom lip. This may suggest some discomfort or disagreement with what you are proposing. We may see abrupt movement. The customer or client may move away from us. Sometimes, we may see the stroking of the chin. They often accompany this by a looking up with the eyes as they enter internal picture mode.

Keep quiet

It is critical that when you observe chin stroking and looking up that you remained silent and say nothing! Wait until the chin stroking is finished and the customer or client begins to speak.

At this point, the customer or client may come back and query the price that you have quoted. Here we can use a very powerful body language technique without actually saying anything. This is the wince. This involves a sharp intake of breath, screwing up the face slightly and moving the head to one side. It is so powerful that you don't even have to say anything. Poor negotiators who are not aware of the wince will immediately start backing down and either start giving away their margin or coming closer to your price.

It is also important at this point that you do not display body language cues that somebody else could pick up on. Be very careful not to put your tongue between your teeth, as this can indicate that you have just got away with something. Also, resist the temptation to rub your hands slowly. It is perfectly fine to display excitement, but this needs to be contained. Too much of a display of excitement can cause buyers remorse.

Be aware that if you have just landed a big deal, where you have managed to get a big margin, there is a temptation as soon as you are out of earshot of the customer or client, to raise your hands in the air and shout "Yes!" Remember that there are other people in the building such as secretaries and receptionists who may pick up on this.

Lastly, be very careful even when you have left the building, as I have heard of some customers who will watch carefully as people leave the building. Any dancing around, high fives or exuberant behaviour could cause any potential deal to collapse. It is much better to do your celebrations when you are fully out of sight and earshot.

Let me entertain you

Sometimes, we meet with customers or clients outside the office. I'm a big proponent of doing this. Going to a neutral venue changes the client customer dynamic. If you can share something pleasurable, like an enjoyable meal or a coffee, then this makes for a more relaxed and informal meeting.

Many people don't even think about which seat is best for a customer when selling or negotiating. If you are taking a client or customer out for lunch, or a coffee, always allow them to sit with their back to the wall. The back is the one area of the body that we cannot protect properly. People will unconsciously feel slightly on edge and their heart rate will rise if their back is exposed. Always allow the client or customer to see where the exit point is. This was reinforced in a recent conversation with someone who admitted to always having to know where the exit is, or he feels uneasy. This tends to be a male trait.

A way to do this is to direct the customer and say, *"Why don't you have this seat?"* If you have a big deal that you wish to work on, book ahead at the restaurant and select a particular table. It is often worthwhile to get to know a restaurant so that you can have your "usual table." These may seem like minor points, but it is important to stack as much as we can in our favour.

CHAPTER 18

In Healthcare

Nonverbal communication is critical within the medical profession and for therapists. Many people involved in the medical profession are unaware of the effect that they have on other people's thinking. We have heard of bedside manner with doctors. It has been documented that it is not only the effects of a drug administered to a patient that affects the patient's belief, but also the doctor's belief in the drug itself. For details of this please consult the author's work in the book "Inside the Mind of Sales."

Human beings are hard-wired for many biases and one of the most powerful of these is a deference to a higher authority. Human beings are generally quite lazy. Henry Ford famously said,

"Thinking is the hardest work there is, which is probably the reason so few engage in it."

In many cases, people would rather outsource their thinking to somebody perceived as an expert than to think for themselves.

One way that we can convey expertise and authority is through a recognised uniform. This explains why doctors wear white coats and why judges and the clergy wear robes. This principle is so important that it can be illustrated in the experiment conducted by Stanley Milgram, a Yale University Psychologist, back in 1953. The experiment tested obedience to authority. It measured the willingness of men from a diverse range of occupations with varying levels of education, to obey an authority figure. The authority figure instructed them to perform acts that conflicted with their conscience. Participants were led to believe that they were assisting an unrelated experiment, in which they had to administer electric shocks to a "learner". While the shocks were fake, the participants were told that they were real. These fake electric shocks were gradually increased to levels that would have been fatal. The experiment found, unexpectedly, that a very high proportion of subjects would fully obey the instructions knowing the fatal doses of electricity were being administered, albeit reluctantly.

Therefore, if you work in the medical profession, realise that this is an authority position and that the nonverbal communication that you are projecting is consistent and congruent. Research into the placebo effect backs this up. Remember, people who come to see you are not looking for entertainment or a friend, but the solution to a problem or the removal of pain.

We can use body language to build rapport and empathy quickly with patients and clients. One of the easiest ways to do this is to sharpen our awareness. It is worth identifying the personality of the client or patient by interpreting their body language. If somebody comes to see you and they are nervous or upset, then it doesn't build a lot of rapport if your body language is one of exuberance.

It is important to not only establish confidence and authority but also to mirror back to the patient or client that you are in rapport with them. It is worth calming down any exuberant gestures. Leaning slightly forward when speaking to the client or patient and slightly lowering your head shows a mark of respect for them. The by-product of angling your head slightly forward is that your voice softens and your vocal pace slows. Suspending judgement is important, as nobody likes to be judged or sneered at. Your nonverbal communication should be one of listening and not "solution mode." Slightly angling the head to one side as discussed previously gives the impression of listening and periodic nodding shows that you understand what the client or patient is saying. Mirroring the body language builds rapport. Depending on the therapy or treatment that you are providing, very often the client does not have a clue what the problem is but wants to be listened to.

If you have a patient or client who is very extroverted and confident, then you can reflect this demeanour to them, which builds rapport.

The power of suggestion is such an important phenomenon and can be used through priming. Priming can be used to alter the environment that you are working in. Simply displaying certificates or diplomas on the walls within easy sight of a patient has a profound priming and suggestive effect. Research discovered by Robert Cialdini showed that certificates of expertise, when displayed on the wall, resulted in a higher compliance rate for an exercise programme, devised by the physiotherapists.

Testimonials or articles being made available in the waiting room before the patient or client meets with you forms another type of priming. It reinforces authority and expertise. The choice of music that you used to play in the background will also have a priming effect on people. Classical music makes people relax, while rock music causes the heart rate to speed up. Some audios take this a stage further and have music tuned to 432Hz. Some think that this is a more natural tuning.

If you are a therapist or hypnotist, your work begins a long way before you even start the therapy or hypnosis. The power of suggestion is such that the patient has to believe that you are competent and have the requisite experience to conduct the therapy or hypnosis. It is critical if you are involved in any of the medical professions, are a therapist or a hypnotist, that you have an environment that is conducive to the treatment that you are providing. Many stage hypnotists will not conduct hypnosis outside the stage environment. They are fully aware of context driven outcomes. Even the act of a hypnotherapist wearing a white coat in an environment akin to a medical centre will create suggestibility. Stage hypnotists know well that the show begins, long before the audience gets anywhere near the theatre.

Seating positions

Having a patient seated at 90 degrees to you, rather than directly opposite, removes barriers. If you are a hypnotist or a therapist with a client or patient and speak to someone from the side, rather than from the front is more effective.

Again, the language helps us out here, "squaring up" is the position we would take in a combative situation.

CHAPTER 19

When Online

With digital technology advancing, more and more people are conducting meetings virtually. Despite the convenience and access to the global markets, one disadvantage of online meetings is that you don't get to see all of a person's body language. We know that the feet and legs give away a lot of clues. The challenge is that these are not in sight when we are online. I often get comments that it would be great if we could read body language online.

Well, we can! We just need to fine-tune our awareness to focus on the upper half of the body. This means that we pay more attention to clues and gestures that we are getting from the shoulders up.

It also becomes harder to mirror somebody when you are speaking to them in a virtual capacity. Nonetheless, there are things you can do to influence people.

People are always communicating, even when they're not communicating. There are clues we can pick up on. If somebody is working from home and they have a backdrop with a large bookcase, this may show that they are an avid reader. When we are building rapport, we want to comment on things that are common to us in our external environment. If the background is very neat and everything is in its place, this can give us a clue about the person.

We can read and use body language online by focusing primarily on the head and the face. The first thing to do is to focus on the image that you are seeing on the screen. What are the first impressions that you get when you are looking at somebody for the first time? I do this quickly and a lot of it goes on at an unconscious level. Let's go through the steps though, so we can identify these consciously.

The background

There are two different scenarios. One is where somebody is online from their place of work and the other is when they are online from another location. Companies are very careful when they design offices to make sure that they create the right impression.

Your home is your castle

When working from home, employers cannot control the background. This means that if somebody is conducting a video call from home, we are getting a view of their environment. From this, we can glean more information. Pay particular attention to the background. Is the background tidy or is it messy? What else do you see in the background that you could use to start a conversation? Small talk usually starts with a comment about an observation in the environment that you can both experience. The classic is a comment about the weather, particularly if you are used to living in a country where the weather changes a lot.

Perhaps you may see a picture in the background you could ask about. I have asked several people about pictures that I have seen in the background. People tend to put up pictures of things they like or are proud of. In one instance, I mentioned a picture in the background and was told that the person had painted it themselves. So much so that once I had mentioned it, they started talking about it at length. You may see a large bookcase which may give a clue that the person likes to read. A comment such as, "it looks like you're an avid reader", or "what is your favourite book", can start a conversation. If there is furniture in the room, is it traditional or new? What are the colours of the walls in the room? Does this show that the person may be more traditional or artistic? There may be a musical instrument in the background. It's just a matter of sharpening our awareness and asking questions to get people engaged. These pieces of information all give us a clue as to the person who we are speaking to.

Real or virtual

If you find you cannot have a backdrop that is in line with the image that you want to portray, it's worth considering getting a green screen. A green screen enables you, depending on the software that you're using, to choose your virtual backdrop. This enables you to prime your customers and clients. Priming is an unconscious process where exposure to external stimuli affects people's thinking and actions. If we want people to make careful assessments, we can show them a picture of Auguste Rodin's "The Thinker." If we want them to be achievement-oriented, we can provide them with an image of a runner winning a race. Priming enables you to influence someone's thinking just based on the image that you have portrayed in the background. In simple terms, think carefully about the image that you choose for the background. I have seen people on video calls switch on a virtual background. It does change the perception that you have of them as the cluttered room disappears. I have also seen some very poor choices.

There are several green screens and they come in a variety of types. Some attach to the back of your chair which is very convenient, some are of the pop-up variety. If you don't wish to buy a green screen, you can make your own by getting some green cloth and attaching it to the wall. Another alternative is to simply paint a piece of plywood green, or attach a green cloth to it. Depending upon the environment and the situation, you may or may not choose to use a green screen or virtual background.

Clothes

Clothes are incredibly important, as they convey an image to other people. Some people may say that clothes don't matter, however, clothes are important. The fashion industry would not be worth billions of dollars each year if they didn't. If clothes don't matter, let's consider attending a black-tie event where most people are wearing a dinner suit or a tuxedo. If you turn up wearing flip-flops, shorts and a tee-shirt, what impression does that give to other people? Like it or not, the brain does judge books by their covers and learns by association. This can be a hindrance at times, but it is also a useful feature. We don't want to learn every day that putting our hand into a fire is painful!

Marketers and businesses know the power of images and its effect on people. We have discussed the influence that a lab coat or robes can have on people in our chapter dealing with medical professionals. The same principle applies to our choice of clothing. When I was younger, I frequently popped into supermarkets, or stores, to pick up a few things whilst wearing a suit. I had several incidences of people asking me questions about the store assuming that I was the manager!

I'm not advocating that you have to wear a suit and tie when interacting with clients or customers online. Your choice of clothing should reflect the image that you wish to portray in your line of business. Would you want to invest millions of dollars with a stockbroker who is wearing an Iron Maiden tee-shirt? Perhaps you may?

When training or coaching people online in a corporate environment, I always wear a shirt. Despite my love for rock music, the tour tee-shirts stay in the closet. If, for example, you are training people on how to use social media platforms, then a jacket and shirt may look too formal. This may seem like common sense and, in many cases, it is. However, it is surprising how few people pay attention to what they are wearing and what the background says about them.

LIGHTS CAMERA ACTION

When we are dealing with people face to face, we don't have to worry about lighting as the human eye compensates. However, when we are communicating via an artificial network such as video, then light becomes much more important. I have been on numerous video calls where the image quality has been low and the lighting has been very poor. We want to stack as many things as we can in our favour with our nonverbal communication. Let's start with lighting.

Lighting

Many people are unaware that their image on the screen is poorly lit or they are sitting against a bright background. This can result in their face being very shadowy. It is possible to invest in a small portable light, preferably with the ability to control the amount of light. If the light appears too harsh, a simple technique of putting paper or toilet tissue over the light diffuses the light to make it softer. This is a relatively cheap investment and will massively improve how you look. It will improve the image that you portray, particularly if you are a figure of authority. Think about the language again when people describe things they are not keen on. The phrase "dark and dingy" gives us a clue. We are naturally attracted to things that are bright and colourful. Perhaps the cosmetic industry knows something?

Camera

Before you switch your camera on, pay particular attention to what is going on in the background. I have been on video calls where there has been a messy unmade bed in the background. I was on another video call where the bathroom door was open and the toilet was on view.

Many people use cameras from their phones, tablets or a computer. Some of these are good, but some of these have a low resolution image. It is possible to buy external high-definition cameras. We can add these to devices and many have the benefit of having software to fine-tune the size of the image on the screen. When working online, the ideal position for the camera is at eye height. A simple box under your device is the pro's secret! Think about the language again. We talk about "looking down at somebody" so we need to be careful about camera position. Ideally, the camera should be as close to the centre of the screen as possible and there should be space for a fist above your head.

There is a potential problem when the camera is at the top of the screen. It means that if you are looking into the camera, you cannot look at the screen and gauge audience interest. This makes it difficult to read the nonverbal signals that the audience give out. This is a dilemma, as people prefer eye contact. The best way to deal with this is to address it before the meeting starts. I simply say that ideally, I should be speaking straight into the camera and then look into the camera and say "just like this." I then explain that if I look into the camera, then I cannot see them properly. I explain that I would prefer to be able to see them, so please forgive me for not looking straight into the camera. This can play in our favour. If there is an important point or message that we want to communicate. Simply by looking straight into the camera at that point we can use analogue marking. Analogue marking is where we can create importance for a particular meaning by changing subtly the way we deliver it. In this case, the viewers will pick up that the point is important every time you speak directly into the camera and not look at the screen.

One thing to avoid is having the camera to one side. I've been in a few video calls where I was seeing a partial side profile of the person that I was speaking to. Not only is this off-putting, but at an unconscious level, it conveys disengagement. We look at things that we like and we look away from things that we don't.

Sounding good

As this book is designed to focus on nonverbal communication and body language, verbal communication is largely out of the scope of this book. One quick mention, though, is to make sure that the way you sound is congruent to the way you look. It is worth being mindful of this and considering investing in an external microphone or a headset.

FIRST IMPRESSIONS

The first thing to pay attention to when seeing somebody on a video call is how tense do they appear. What is the first impression that you have of them? Does their face look tense? Do they look nervous? What sort of mood are they in? Are they smiling a lot and how willing are they to engage in eye contact? Is their head looking up or is it looking down? If you are presenting to a group of people, this is a useful skill to develop. If you are presenting for the first time in a meeting, it is always good to identify who are the "friends," and who are the likely "foes." The "friends" will usually help and interact, while the foes can be difficult. What happens through herding is that when some people interact online, then others like to join in too.

Heads first

People who are listening to what you're saying tend to tilt their heads slightly to one side. When people are agreeing with what you're saying, you will often see some unconscious nodding and this can be very subtle. If we agree with somebody, simply tilting our head to one side and starting to nod gently gives the impression that we are in agreement and paying attention. We want to make this a visible action without looking silly.

Head support

Somebody who is supporting their head while you are speaking, particularly if there has been a change in position that they have adopted, can indicate boredom. (Chapter 8)

This is not to be confused with somebody whose hand is on the side of their face. If the hand is on the side of the face, be aware of the thumb position. If the thumb is under the chin, this might indicate a disagreement with what you're saying.

Eyebrows

Somebody's eyebrows can show whether they are surprised or not. People raise their eyebrows in surprise. If somebody is presenting online and displays surprise, you may see the eyebrows raise. We can show our surprise by raising our eyebrows too. We have already covered the eyebrow flash as a greeting mechanism and this can be used effectively in online meetings, too.

The eyebrows can also show concentration and the seriousness of something. Simply lowering your eyebrows slightly and moving your head slightly forward while nodding will show to the other person that you appreciate the seriousness of the situation and that you agree. Remember, we want to appear congruent, and a big beaming smile with raised eyebrows at a serious moment does not convey this.

The lips

The lips can be very useful to pay attention to. A narrowing of the lips can show a disagreement with what you are saying. The disappearance of the lower lip and any form of biting can indicate discomfort or disagreement with what you are saying. Pay particular attention to the pursing of the lips. (Chapter 10)

This can mean that somebody wants to hold back what they are thinking. In a normal position, you would expect to see both the lips. Be very careful to make sure that your lips don't narrow and try to avoid the pursed lip position.

The eyes

A narrowing of the eyes together with a lowering of the eyebrows, while listening to you, can indicate suspicion. Pupils dilate when we see something that we like and constrict when we see something that we don't. This is difficult to pick up when we are online unless the person is very close to the camera.

Blinking

Blinking is mostly out of our conscious awareness, both our own and the blink rate of others. Simply blinking at the same rate as somebody while online will unconsciously set up a link between you and them. I have noticed that many people, particularly intellectuals, when thinking or pontificating very often increase their blink rate. This seems to occur when they are in deep thought.

Measuring the energy

A key thing to measure before you start your meeting is the energy level within the group or the individual that you're speaking to. There is nothing worse than a mismatch in energy. Ideally, we want to have our energy at a slightly higher level than those around us. I'm sure many of us have had the experience of the game show host, where somebody is just far too energetic. Remember, we want to pace and lead our audience. That means adopting a slightly higher energy level than the group and then increasing it as the meeting goes on. Being too energetic when someone has just received bad news is a mismatch.

If you are speaking to a group of people in a meeting for the first time each group dynamic is different. Pay particular attention to any tension in people's faces. Look out also for those who appear friendly or relaxed. Also, make a mental note of those who appear withdrawn or introverted as you will need to work harder with those. Some groups are less interactive than others. The way to increase the level of engagement is to ask those, who are more reserved, a series of open, (who when why where what and how), questions.

The key to analysing and influencing using body language and nonverbal communication online is to really sharpen your awareness and observe closely.

.

CHAPTER 20

Presenting & Public Speaking

There are two aspects to be aware of with body language and nonverbal communication when presenting and public speaking.

1. Being aware of your audience's body language.

2. Being aware of your body language to increase your skill as a public speaker.

When standing in front of people, there is a lot to be aware of with your nonverbal communication. The best way to practise is to break it down into small chunks. Let's start with the overall image that we want to portray. Everybody has their own presenting style and we must be comfortable. We don't want to be someone else. As I've stated throughout this book, and in other books, the most effective way to control and utilise your body language effectively is to manage your state.

Let's start by looking at the legs. As discussed, the legs and the feet are the most honest part of the body. (Chapter 5) They are the hardest to disguise and will leak signals. You can learn with practice to control your legs and feet. The best way to practise this is to stand in front of the mirror and to have your feet about 18 inches or 45 centimetres apart. They can be slightly flared or pointing at the audience. It's important to have your weight equally balanced on both legs. You can enhance this by imagining that your feet are set in concrete. When I was first learning to present and speak in public, I put more weight on one leg than the other. This didn't convey confidence and was certainly not a powerful pose. The way to practise this is to get in position, then move away and do it again. Keep moving so that it becomes automatic. Now that we have our feet in position, it's also important that we don't start rocking, shifting or crossing our legs. (Chapter 5)

The torso

We need control any pelvic gyration and make sure that our body is facing the audience. If you stand away from the lectern, this conveys a more open, confident and trusting impression. This may be uncomfortable for some. When speaking, it is important to move around the speaking area, as the eye is naturally attracted to movement and this helps maintain a connection and interest for the audience.

The hands can convey your message more effectively. Research by Holler and Beatie, found that gestures increase the value of someone's message by 60 per cent. People often don't know what to do with their hands and arms when speaking in public. It's largely because they become consciously aware of them when nervous. A good rule of thumb is to have your hands down by your side in a relaxed manner. Be mindful to not fidget with your fingers as this is distracting for the audience. Then just follow the six second rule and raise your hands after speaking for about six seconds.

My preference is not to have my hands in my pockets, as I think it looks either too casual or lacking in confidence. If you are putting your hands in your pockets, be careful that you don't suffer from "active hands." We want to avoid "pocket snooker" or "pocket pool." Remember to keep your hands on full display and avoid putting them into your back pockets. This is a classic sign of nervousness that is displayed by inexperienced speakers. The hiding of thumbs in the pockets is another display of lack of confidence. (Chapter 7)

Lending a hand

We can use our arms and hands to help add expression to our presentation. Honesty and openness can be conveyed by making sure that we show the audience the palms of our hands and by avoiding pointing. We can also use our hands to emphasise key points in our message to drive the points home. This is better done without clenched fists. We can emphasise good points with one hand and problem areas with another.

The head

Holding your head up and looking straight ahead is a sign of confidence. If you are engaging with the audience, tilting your head to one side shows that you're listening and nodding indicates that you agree. We can also use nodding to accentuate the meaning of an important point. If for example, you said it's absolutely critical that we pay attention to "abc" and start nodding while you say this, will have more effect than just stating the point on its own.

Eye contact is very important and is an area where inexperienced speakers let themselves down. They either don't look at the audience, or they look at only one small section of the audience, which makes others feel alienated. It is a skill that takes practice. One of the easiest ways to do this is to divide the audience into quarters and to make sure that you are looking around at each quarter randomly.

Smile

Remember to smile with a genuine smile. Make sure to look as if you're pleased to be presenting or speaking.

Compliance

A powerful technique that a lot of entertainers and presenters use is compliance. The principle is that if people accept one suggestion, then they are more predisposed to follow the next. This helps to build rapport with the audience and gets them to follow instructions. Often, this starts with something physical. It may involve them standing up, raising their hands in the air, or clapping. If, as the presenter, you clap when someone does or answers a question then the audience will take this as a cue to join in. This is the first stage in getting an audience or group to be on your side.

Controlling the energy

It is important to match the energy of the audience with our delivery. Ideally, we want to have more energy than the audience without appearing over the top. This energy can be controlled depending on the feedback that we get from the audience. We can vary this using movement and gestures.

CHAPTER 21

Attraction & Seduction

The book so far has focussed on how we can use body language and nonverbal communication in everyday life and business situations. I hesitated before adding a chapter on attraction and courtship. This is largely because of the complexity and different types of relationships that exist. It is also difficult and impossible to cover every single scenario. The published research (see references) is largely based on heterosexual relationships. As this book focuses on scientific evidence, we will focus on this types of relationships in this chapter. That being said, many of the principles hold true for other types of relationships.

We generate much of nonverbal communication from hardwired emotions. While many people may not be looking for a potential partner, I would hazard a guess that this chapter will not be skipped. The desire to procreate is a strong hard-wired behaviour in human beings. There are distinct patterns of behaviour that show this. We only have to look at the amount of money spent on making ourselves look more attractive through clothes, cosmetics, fragrances, and accessories, together with a drive for power, to see this in action.

Business & customer attraction

Despite my hesitation to cover this topic, there is a need to identify the signals in business and everyday situations. This prevents any awkward, inappropriate or conflict of interests that may result. We have all seen instances where business or relationships have developed further and with it added complications.

Making it simple

In this section, for simplicity, we will cover the body language and nonverbal communications in a heterosexual relationship. However, by paying attention to the signals, many are interchangeable, depending on the type of relationship that you are in. With all this in mind, let's get started.

ATTRACTING SOMEONE'S ATTENTION

Physiological changes occur when someone comes into contact with a member of the opposite sex with whom they are attracted. According to researcher Dr Albert Scheflen, muscle tone in the torso, arms, legs, and face all tighten up. The walking becomes more fluid and bouncy. Men stand taller. They jut out their chins, push out their chests, and pull in their stomachs. Women tilt their heads to the side, engage in hair display signals, and expose their wrists and necks in a dismissive pose. The pupils dilate also dilate. Pupil dilation is out of conscious control. It happens automatically.

Women give most signals out and these are context driven. For example, if you go to traditional places where flirting takes place, such as singles bars and nightclubs, you will see familiar patterns of behaviour going on. These would be very different to the behaviours displayed when meeting somebody during the day in a typical environment, such as in the work environment or while out shopping.

Attraction

There is a common misconception that men are the initiators when it comes to dating. The vast majority of the time it is women who are the ones to give off the signals first, and the research supports this.

MEN AND WOMEN

When women are ovulating, research shows they are more likely to display more skin, wear shorter skirts and higher heels. They also act more provocatively. During this time, some behaviours covered in the next section may be exaggerated.

Many signals are given out at an unconscious level. Many women may not even realise that they are giving out signals and may not realise why men are approaching them. These signals can be subtle too. Women are generally better at reading nonverbal communication and body language signals than men. This has been suggested for years and now the science has substantiated this. Consider a scenario of two couples meeting for dinner. During dinner, the woman may spot that the other couple's relationship is not going well. She may highlight this to her husband or partner. He will usually reply, that they seemed to be getting on pretty well to him. Then, within a month, the other couple split up, and the man is stunned. He then states that he never saw this coming.

Picking up on the signals

Signals involved in courtship and attraction are complicated and extensive. As women give out more signals, there will be more of an emphasis on the female signals to help men interpret and recognise these better. However, this will benefit women too. Raising the awareness of the signals that are being given out, many of which are unconscious, enables these to be dialled up or dialled down accordingly.

Research conducted in 2008 by Dr. Coreen Farris of Indiana University shows that men just don't get it when it comes to sexual signals. Most men are not very good at picking up on subtle signals. They often misread signals. Men often get confused with the difference between flirting and friendly behaviour. I am sure many of the females reading this book will identify with this. For many men, approaching a woman is a big thing. There is always the risk of rejection or ridicule. Some men don't even bother looking for signals. They will just approach a woman out of the blue. This can often have disastrous results. Many just play the numbers game.

The trick is for men to sharpen their awareness and to learn the signals covered in this book. For women, the trick is to make the signals more obvious that they are interested. If women can improve the clearness of their signals, and men can learn to read the signals, then this is mutually beneficial for both men and women.

Men prefer a direct approach. If women are aware of the signals and communicate these clearly, men will respond. From a woman's point of view, they can sometimes get frustrated that the man is not picking up on what they see are obvious signals. If a woman wants to send attraction signals out, it is better to be obvious rather than being subtle. In simple terms, think of men as switches and women as dials. The best way to think about this is to use the example of a volume control on a music player. If the music is too quiet, turn the volume up. We can use this analogy too when sending out attraction signals. If the man is not picking up the signals, intensify the signal gradually. After all, if the music is too quiet, we don't suddenly turn the volume up. We increase it until at a comfortable level. If the signal is not being picked up, simply turn it up until the switch gets flicked.

Men are often caught in the trap of not wanting to misread signals. It is best therefore for men, once they pick up on one signal, to not go in all guns blazing but to allow the female to send out more signals.

ATTRACTION SIGNALS

Context driven

Dr Monica Moore of the University of Missouri conducted a study of how women interacted in public. Eighteen to thirty-five-year-old women in singles bars were followed and studied. Two interesting results were observed.

1. The flirting was location specific. Most of the flirting occurred in singles bars and was virtually non-existent in other locations.
2. The second major finding was that men approached women who signalled the most. However, when men sent out signals, they failed at receiving attention from women.

Another study found that up to 70% of all courtship is initiated by women. They also found that more attractive females showing fewer signals attracted less attention. Therefore, if you want to get more attention, dial up the signals, and dial them down if you don't. It's not that much more complicated than that.

Some women may have experienced a situation when they have been out for a night out with a friend. The sole purpose of which was to meet up, have fun, and catch up. They then find that a man approaches them and it becomes annoying. Their conversation is interrupted and their space is invaded by an unwanted approach. This is why it is so important for men to be able to read the signals and to avoid having to put themselves in a difficult situation.

POWERFUL PRINCIPLES

When analyzing attraction signals, the same principles apply as they do for body language reading.

The fundamental principle

"The outer expression is a reflection of the inner thought, and gestures should not be taken in isolation."

The first principle

"We move towards things that we like and we move away from things that we don't."

People who are attracted to each other will be closer to each other. This degree of closeness will reflect the attraction. For most of us, if there is somebody that we don't like or that we do not get on with, we tend to "keep well out of their way." We do this by avoiding verbal communication and being seen. If somebody is keeping their distance, then they do not feel attracted to you.

The second principle

"We look at things that we like and we look away from things that we don't like."

If we like somebody, we will hold their gaze a fraction longer. Have you ever noticed, with somebody you don't like and with whom you don't feel you're on the same wavelength, how much harder it is to hold eye contact with them?

The third principle

"The body and the head will point towards people that we are attracted to."

This is evident with the actions of the feet. (Chapter5)

The fourth principle

"We open up physically to people that we like and we close down to people that we don't like."

An example of this is how much information you share with somebody that you don't like? This applies physically too.

The final principle

"Asymmetrical body language accompanies attraction"

This is obvious in environments such as bars and nightclubs. Advertisers and the fashion industry know the power of asymmetry. (Chapter 22)

Sharpening your awareness and becoming more aware of these principles will assist you when assessing if somebody is attracted to you or not. The challenge arises because human behaviour is complicated. Different people have different degrees of awareness of their environment. For some people, things have to be fairly obvious. For others, they pick up on things fairly quickly. The good news is that it is possible to develop your awareness skills.

THE BIG RULE

The "Big Rule" is that none of the following patterns in isolation should be taken to mean one thing. We will go through some patterns of behaviour so that you can learn what to look for. We will break this down into smaller pieces. For many of you, this may be learning a new skill. Ideally, we want to read these patterns and for them to become unconscious

The best way to learn a new skill is to narrow your focus and start to recognise things that occur during an interaction and to sharpen your awareness. Trying to focus on everything at once can become confusing. Developing your communication skills takes time and practice. Commit to observing up to two patterns at a time and your awareness will soon sharpen up. Many of the patterns of behaviour that we will discuss are context-driven. This means that they are exaggerated in environments where you would normally expect to see attraction occur, such as in singles bars or nightclubs.

SUBMISSION

Submission is a fundamental principle when analysing female body language in an attraction situation and this comes from the published research. It is important to emphasise that we are referring to attraction patterns and not in any way referring to inequality or dominance in other areas of life. The research shows that the nonverbal signals women give out are submissive signals in an attraction situation. This evokes a basic protective response in men. Remember that we are dealing with primal drivers from the very primitive part of the brain. This is in no way saying that women should be submissive to men. As we discussed in the chapter about the brain, we are dealing with very basic hard-wired emotions that help human beings find a partner to procreate with. Let's look at this principle in more detail and, of course, there are going to be exceptions.

SEXUAL DIFFERENCES

Women tend to prefer men who are bigger, taller and more dominant and the research shows this. Men prefer women that show submissive postures. The language again gives us a clue, "being swept off her feet."

The bottom line is that when a person wants to attract the opposite sex, they emphasise sexual differences. These differences are exaggerated through clothes, cosmetics, accessories and behaviour in an attraction environment.

To discourage the opposite sex, we play down or hide these differences. This can be useful to know so that we can either encourage interaction or discourage unwanted advances. It also allows us to recognise the patterns in other relationships and to spot any potential conflict interests. Let's work our way through the various body language signals that are given out, starting with the feet.

FOOT DISPLAY

Pigeon toes

Fig.120

Fig.121

Tibial Torsion is a submissive foot display and is better known as pigeon toes. "Pigeon toes" refers to aiming the toes and feet inward at a slight angle. (Fig.120) We can often see this in typical environments where people would go to meet other people such as singles bars or nightclubs. The opposite of this is where the legs are splayed and the feet are pointing out. We often associate leg splay with policemen or military personnel. (Fig.121) I have noticed that some female police officers also adopt this position. Women in courtships take up submissive displays to attract the attention of men. We've already discussed in the section on personality types that dominant people make themselves bigger and take up more space. Adopting the pigeon toes position by many females makes them appear smaller and come across as less threatening.

Shoe fondle

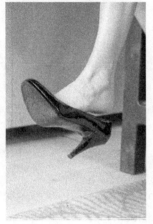

Fig.122

The "shoe fondle" occurs where the foot is dangled by the toes and bobbed up and down. (Fig.122) This can show comfort but also acts as a flirtatious signal. This is a more extreme version of the shoe dangle seen in a business environment. This display is context drive and more likely to be seen in environments where attracting a partner is the goal.

LEGS

Fig.123

There are some nonverbal displays that we can look for with the legs. (Fig.123) Most men agree that the "leg twine" is the most appealing seated position that a woman can adopt. We see one leg firmly pressed against the other. This gives an appearance of high muscle tone. Other leg signals used by women include crossing and uncrossing the legs slowly in front of the man and gently stroking the thighs with her hand.

The knee point

Fig.124

The knee point occurs where one leg is tucked under the other and points to the person that is the most attractive or most interesting. This occurs in men and women. (Fig.124)

LIPS

Fig.125

Lip licking can be a clue of sexual interest. This must be looked at in context and the overall pattern of behaviour. If you are in a meeting and the chief executive is presenting and she licked her lips, it would be highly unlikely that this would be conceived as a sexual gesture. Lip licking can be a clue of sexual interest, but only if there are other clues. (Fig.125) One nonverbal display in isolation only gives us a clue that needs to be investigated further. For example, lip licking can be a habit. We normally associate this as a female trait and flirting signal. I once worked with somebody who had a habit of licking his lips. This was purely a habit and was not suggestive. It is not the act in isolation, but what accompanies it that will give you a clue as to the meaning.

NECK

Fig.126

A woman exposes her neck to make herself look appealing. She can either raise her chin slightly or turn her head to the side to expose her neck. Women sometimes stroke their necks, which is a sign of interest. When the indentation at the base of the neck is shown, we associate it with submission and approachability. A man who loosens his tie in the presence of another woman may be unknowingly expressing his attraction. (Fig.126) I remember speaking to a woman once who was telling me about a date that she had been on. She said, "I knew as soon as the tie was removed that it was on!"

EYES

The principle with the eyes is that we look at things that we like and look away from things that we don't. The pupils are one part of the body over which we have no conscious control. As such, they are a reliable indicator that someone likes what they see. They dilate when we see someone to whom we are attracted. They constrict when we see people we dislike.

This was known by prostitutes from years gone by who would dilate their pupils through the use of Belladonna, which contains atropine.

HIPS

Rolling hips

Fig.127

Women naturally have wider hips than men and have a wider gap between their legs. (Fig.127) Women can emphasise their hips with an accentuated roll of the pelvic region. This walk is called the "parade." This happens when a woman walks with exaggerated swinging or rolling of the hips. The head is held high, and the back is arched, and the chest is pressed out. Hip emphasis is seen in the fashion industry with the walk on the catwalk. In advertising, we see women with weight placed on one side with the hips forced out to exaggerate the curves. Research has shown that women who are not in a committed relationship unconsciously walk in this manner to attract attention.

HEAD AND SHOULDERS

The face frame

Fig. 128

This is a gesture used in courtship and attraction. We discussed earlier that head support is a demonstration of boredom or disinterest. The "face frame" or "face platter" is different. (Fig.128) Women use it to attract a man's attention. A woman will place one hand on top of the other as if framing the face for the man to admire. The head is lightly supported but does not require significant support. This is unlike the boredom sign when the head is heavily supported or has thumb support.

The head tilt

The head tilt shows sexual interest. It is slightly different to the listening tilt as the head is tilted backwards to expose the neck. (Fig.129) This can often be accompanied by looking over a raised shoulder and playing with the hair.

Fig.129

Room glance

This is a pattern of eye behaviour and is used to attract the attention of men. This is an unconscious response, but it does follow a sequence. To begin with, the woman looks or scans the room. (Fig.130) This is context-driven and usually takes place in a bar, club, or an event where there are lots of members of the opposite sex.

This first glance is a scan to see who is there and what is going on. It satisfies

Fig.130

her curiosity. This is not a sexual cue, but is the equivalent of window shopping. If the woman sees someone that she is attracted to, she will quickly move her eyes downward. This is to show submission. She will then take a second look at the man that she is interested in and will then look away after two to five seconds. This pattern of behaviour is repeated until the man picks up on the signal.

Forehead bow

The "forehead bow," or looking up through the forehead, is a submissive posture. (Fig.131) The forehead bow is done by lowering the head, then looking up at a man from under the eyebrows. This is often accompanied by a tilting the head to one side, which makes the look easier to do.

Fig.131

HAIR PLAY

Fig.132

Fig.133

The Head Toss and Hair Flick

This is often one of the first displays that a woman will use around someone that she is attracted to after the initial eye contact. The head is tossed back, and the hair is tossed over the shoulders and from the face. (Fig.132) This exposes the neck. This gesture is used by women with short hair too. This is often associated with other hair gestures, such as running the fingers through the hair in a preening gesture. The hair may also be curled around the fingers and wrapped around the neck.

Sometimes women will use a "fish and lure" tactic. This is an unconscious response. This happens in the absence of eye contact with a particular individual. There is a general look around the room and a flick of the hair. (Fig.133) Often this is accompanied by hair play or hair preening to show that she has arrived and wants attention. We see this in singles bars. We should not see any hair play in isolation but as part of attraction clusters. Hair play can also be a comforting gesture.

Shoulder raises

The single shoulder raise narrows the body and creates asymmetry, which we associate with the body language of attraction. (Fig.134) This is often accompanied by a lowering of the head. The rise of the shoulder is slower and often held for longer than a typical shoulder shrug.

Fig.134

HANDS AND ARMS

Touch too much

The hands can give away attraction signs through the open display of palms. This is often accompanied by a wrist display

Fig.135

which we will cover in the next section. One of the main telltale signals of attraction is the touch, which comes a few stages and later in the process of attraction. At some point, the woman will make contact with the man. (Fig. 135) This can be the briefest of touches and may only be a soft brush, but it will take place. Many men are oblivious to the significance of this.

Types of contact

There are several types of contact to look out for. The woman

Fig.136

may lean forward and touch the man's knee if he has been teasing her with a comment. She may also pick some thread or lint from his clothing. (Fig.136) We also see a touching on the back of the hand, the forearm or the upper arm. There may be a soft brush against the man. Sometimes if the man is wearing a tie, she may straighten his tie. Many of these gestures are subtle.

Once this touch has taken place, the woman has given permission to be touched back in the same way. For the men reading this, it means a light touch in return and not a grab. We will look at this in the stages of courtship later.

WRISTS

The limp wrist

This can be seen while walking or sitting. The limp wrist is a submission signal used by heterosexual women. (Fig.137) The limp wrist is a gesture adopted by women and those wanting to appear more effeminate. Care needs to be taken in a business situation because it can weaken credibility.

Fig. 137   Fig. 138

Exposed Wrists

If a woman is interested in a man, she will gradually expose the underside skin of her wrists. This display of the wrist will increase as interest develops. Palm exposure also increases.

The wrist display is often shown by a woman who is smoking. We may see the wrist display when the palms are facing up on the table. Sometimes we see the wrist display when the hair is being stroked or when playing with an earlobe. (Fig.138) The more that the wrists are flashed then the more interest is displayed.

ARMS

Studies reveal that women adopt open arm positions when they are in the company of men that they like. They cross their arms with men that they dislike. This ties in with the language of someone being "closed" and difficult to open up.

FINGERS

Fig.139

Fingers in the mouth can indicate nervousness. However when the head is tilted and we have asymmetrical body language, this can be used as an attractive signal. (Fig.139) We may see a raised shoulder and pigeon toes and some self-touching. This is a submissive pose and appeals to the primal male instincts and to display vulnerability and the need for protection. This occurs at an unconscious level and is rarely seen in everyday settings, being restricted to attraction situations.

SELF TOUCHING

Both sexes use similar preening gestures. This includes touching the hair, smoothing the clothing, hand or hands on the hips and the body, legs and feet pointing to the other person.

Women have dramatically more nerve sensors for experiencing

touch than men. Most pictures of women in sensual poses include plenty of self-touching. Self-touching is an attraction signal that women display more than men. (Fig.140) This is not an overt sexual form but it may take the form of self-touching on the legs, playing with hair or with the hands and wrists. If you doubt the effect of this, just look at any magazine advert, where attraction is the aim and notice how the

Fig.140

hands are positioned and the degree to which self-touching takes place.

SMILING

Women tend to smile more than men and the research backs this up. (Fig.141) This is often through habit or to appease men. Smiling can sometimes be a sexual signal but only if accompanied by other attraction signals as a stack to give more concrete clues. If a woman is smiling and with a sideways glance over a raised shoulder

Fig.141

with pouted lips, this may indicate sexual interest. For a man, it does not mean that because a woman smiled at you she wants to go to bed with you!

BEING PLAYFUL

If you want to appear more attractive come across as more playful. Everyone likes to have fun and while this is not a body language pattern, it is more of a philosophy in the field of attraction.

TIPS FOR FEMALES

Make your signals more obvious for the men that you want to attract and dial down and become aware of any signals that you may give out that may be attraction signals to those men that you are not attracted to.

MALE BODY LANGUAGE

There are fewer male body language signals, and these tend to be more obvious. Men will stare more when they like someone and they tend to have a roving eye. They will also move closer to someone that they like. It is important for males to be aware of the effect that their less subtle body language can have on females. Let's look at some typical examples of male body language.

I'm a cowboy

A classic male attraction pose is with the hands in the belt hoops. Fig. (142) The hands point down to the groin in the cowboy stance. We also see a variation of this with the hands in the pockets and the thumbs on display. (Fig.143) The thumbs protruding from the pockets indicate confidence. These positions may periodically include self-grooming, such as the running of the fingers through the hair.

Fig.142

Fig.143

I need space

Fig.144

Men when trying to appear confident, will often try to make themselves bigger by puffing out their chest, standing taller and engaging in preening gestures such are running their hands through their hair or adjusting their jacket. As discussed earlier, dominant characters will take up more space. In an attraction situation are you making yourself bigger or smaller? Many women like confident men, and this is often shown by taking up more space. (Fig.144)

TIPS FOR MALES

Fig.145   Fig.146

Learn the female body language signals and be aware of your own body language. How are you coming across? Are you confident or apologetic? (Fig.145)

Fig.147   Fig.148

Are you getting too close to her personal space? (Fig.146) Have you had a touch from her? (Fig.147) This could be a light brush, a light touch on the hand or picking something from your clothing. Does she appear interested or bored? (Fig.148)

7 STAGES OF ATTRACTION

Stage 1 Eye contact

A woman looks across the room and sees a man that she is attracted to. She waits until he notices her. She then holds his gaze for between two to five seconds and then turns away and often looks down. When the woman finally gets his attention, we may witness a more compact version of the "Eyebrow Flash." This causes a subtle, eye-widening gesture. This lets the man know that it was intended for him. The man now keeps watching to see if she does it again. This needs to be repeated on average three times before the average man realises that she is interested in him.

Stage 2 Smiling

The woman then gives a brief half-smile. This is a signal that the man has been given permission to approach. Unfortunately, many men are not responsive and do not pick up on these signals and the woman is often left feeling that he is not interested in her.

Stage 3 Preening

She will sit up straight and often will cross and uncross her legs if seated. The body position, even while seated, may be asymmetrical. If the woman is standing, then she tilts her hips and her head sideways. This creates asymmetry within the body. This tilting of the head displays the neck and we may witness some hair playing display. We may also see her lick her lips, and she may flick her hair and her clothes and jewellery may be straightened or adjusted. The man will respond with gestures such as standing up straight, pulling in his stomach in and puffing out his chest with his head raised high.

He may run his fingers through his hair or begin adjusting his clothing. We sometimes see the man put his thumbs in his belt hoop and he walks across with a slight swagger.

Stage 4 Small talk

The man then attempts to make small talk. Depending on his conversational skills and the interest of the woman the conversation continues.

Stage 5 Object moving

At some point, the woman will move an object closer to the man. This is an indication of wanting to become closer. The woman may move her bag closer or her phone closer to him. (Fig.149) If she is drinking and when she places her glass back down, it will be moved closer. These patterns of behaviour are unconscious but are important to look for. This is a sign of attraction.

Fig. 149

Stage 6 Touch

The woman, if interested, will look for an opportunity to initiate a light touch. (Fig.150) This may be designed to look unintentional, but women know that this is anything but accidental. This may be a light touch on the hand, the arm or the shoulder and may be in response to something amusing that the man has said. She may touch him and say that he is so funny. Sometimes the touch can be the lightest of brushes. This may occur as she "accidentally" touches the man as she brushes past him to go to the ladies room. Once the touch has been initiated by the woman, permission has been given for the man to touch back. It is safe to do this in the same place except for the chest area. Men must realise that this means a light touch back and not a grope.

Stage 7 Moving closer

Stage 7 is a progressive phase where unconsciously both the female and the male move closer together. This progressive movement ends up with both being very close. (Fig.151)

These first seven stages of courtship may seem trivial, but they are observable and can give great insights into the level of attraction.

Fig.150

Fig.151

CHAPTER 22

Conclusion

We have covered a great deal of material in this book. I have endeavoured to cover most patterns of nonverbal behaviour that we will come across. We have looked at how to interpret, and how to use these patterns of behaviour in different environments and in doing so, how to understand and influence people. By learning the principles of body language and nonverbal communication, you can learn and spot more of your own. This is the best way.

The best thing about learning body language and nonverbal communication is that it is fun. Meetings become more interesting, as do everyday interactions. The ability to say, I sense that..... or I get the impression that..... is powerful and shows understanding.

Human behaviour is complicated. It must be emphasised that no gesture in isolation should be taken as giving the complete picture. It is merely a part of the puzzle. Much of how we interpret people and form opinions occurs at an unconscious level. This often gives us our intuitions. If we can learn those consciously, it gives us a greater understanding of how some of these intuitions are generated. This gives us a greater chance to understand and re-examine these intuitions.

The study of body language and nonverbal communication is best approached as an ongoing study. Try to develop a natural curiosity and remember to take things in small steps. Start by picking a particular pattern of behaviour and focus on noticing it. Once you can readily identify this pattern, then move on to focussing on another one.

Learning everything at once can appear overwhelming. Think about the chocolate or candy bar the Toblerone. If you were to try and eat it all at once, it would be painful because the chocolate is hard in your mouth. However, breaking it into smaller chunks enables it to be eaten easily.

Practise and start observing people's behaviours in different situations. Look in magazines. What does someone's body language say? Is it congruent with what they are trying to convey? If so, why, and if not, why not? Try watching live television with the sound turned down. What can you spot?

Finally, remember to listen to the audio, which comes with this book, which will help program your mind for success to enable you to learn this skill faster. Repetitive listening will make this more effective. It is enjoyable and is an easy way to learn.

Committing to learning this skill will pay dividends not only in your business, but also in your personal and intimate relationships. People have a fascination with body language. You may even find yourself as the centre of attention, at a gathering, as you display your newfound knowledge.

Don't confine this book to gathering dust, but come back to it frequently and make a conscious decision to master this skill.

Remember, there are none so blind as those that cannot see. You can do it, and I look forward to your success.

Get Your Complimentary

BONUS Rapid Learning Accelerator Audio
&
BONUS Chapter "Seating For Power & Influence"

https://www.howtoreadanybody.com

Thanks for reading this book.
If you enjoyed it then it would be enormously helpful if you would be kind enough to leave a review?
This makes all those early mornings and late nights worthwhile.

Many thanks

For Coaching. Training or Speaking Enquiries
https://www.power2mind.com

Please see the next page for other books by the author

REFERENCES

Acredolo, Linda, and Susan Goodwyn (1985). "Symbolic Gesturing in Language Development: A Case Study." In Human Development (Vol. 28), pp. 40-49.

Aiello, J. 1977. Visual interaction as a function of interpersonal distance. Environmental Psychology & Nonverbal Behavior, 1: 122-140.

Akehurst, Lucy, Gunter Kohnken, Aldert Vrij, and Ray Bull (1996). "Lay Persons and Police Officers Beliefs Regarding Deceptive Behaviour." In Applied Cognitive Psychology (Vol. 10, Issue 6), pp. 461-71.

Allan Mazur; Eugene Rosa; Mark Faupel; Joshua Heller; Russell Leen; Blake Thurman. Physiological Aspects of Communication Via Mutual Gaze. The American Journal of Sociology. 1980; 86(1): 50-74.

Altmann, Stuart (1967). "The Structure of Primate Communication." In Stuart Altmann, ed., Social Communication Among Primates (Chicago: University of Chicago Press), pp. 325-62.

Amato, Ivan (1992). "In Search of the Human Touch." In Science (Vol. 258, 27 November), pp. 1436-437.

Andrew, R. J. (1963). "Evolution of Facial Expression." In Science (Vol. 142), pp. 1034-41.

Andrew, R. J. (1965). "The Origins of Facial Expression." In Scientific American (Vol. 213), pp. 88-94.

Appelbaum, P.S. The new lie detectors: Neuroscience, deception, and the courts. Psychiatric Services. 2007. 58: 460-462.

Argyle, M. 1988. Bodily communication (2nd ed.). London: Methuen.

Argyle, M. and Cook, M. Gaze and Mutual Gaze. London: Cambridge University Press, 1976.

Argyle, M. The Psychology of Interpersonal Behaviour. London: Penguin Books, 1967.

Argyle, M., and Ingham, R. 1972. Gaze, mutual gaze, and proximity. Semiotica, 1, 32–49.

Argyle, Michael; Lefebvre, Luc; Cook, Mark 1974. The meaning of five patterns of gaze.European Journal of Social Psychology. 4(2): 125-136.

Armstrong, David F., William C. Stokoe, and Sherman E. Wilcox (1995). Gesture and the Nature of Language (New York: Cambridge University Press).

Ashton-James, C., R. B. van Baaren, T. L. Chartrand, J. Decety, and J. Karremans. 2007. Mimicry and me: the impact of mimicry on self-construal. Social Cognition 25 (4): 518-535.

Barber N. 1995. The evolutionary psychology of physical attractiveness: sexual selection and human morphology. Ethology and Sociobiology 16: 395-424.

Barinaga, Marcia (1995). "Brain Researchers Speak a Common Language." In Science (Vol. 270, December), pp. 1437-8.

Barinaga, Marcia (1998). "FMRI Provides New View of Monkey Brains." In Science (Vol. 282, November 20), p.1397).

Bateson, Gregory (1955). "A Theory of Play and Fantasy." In Psychiatric Research Reports (Vol. 2), pp.39-59

Bateson, Gregory (1968). "Redundancy and Coding." In Thomas A. Sebeok (Ed.), Animal Communication (Bloomington: Indiana University Press), pp. 614-26.

Baumgartel, Walter (1976). Up Among the Mountain Gorillas (New York: Hawthorn Books).

Beatrice de Gelder. 2006. Towards the neurobiology of emotional body language. Source: Nature reviews. Neuroscience. 7 (3): 242 -249.

Bechara, Antoine, Daniel Tranel, Hanna Damasio, Ralph Adolphs, Charles Rockland, and Antonio R. Damasio (1995). "Double Dissociation of Conditioning and Declarative Knowledge Relative to the Amygdala and Hippocampus in Humans." In Science (Vol. 269, 25 August), pp. 1115-1118.

Beebe, S.A., Beebe, S.J., Redmond, M.V. 2008. Interpersonal Communication: 5th Edition. Boston, MA: Pearson Education.

Berdecio, Susana, and Leanne T. Nash (1981). Chimpanzee Visual Communication: Facial, Gestural and Postural Expressive Movement in Young, Captive Chimpanzees (Pan troglodytes) (Arizona State University: Anthropological Research Papers No. 26).

Birdwhistell, Ray (1952). An Introduction to Kinesics (Louisville: University of Louisville).

Birdwhistell, Ray (1970). Kinesics and Context (Philadelphia: University of Pennsylvania).

Bixler, Susan (1984). The Professional Image (New York: G. P. Putnam's Sons).

Blairy, S., P. Herrera, and U. Hess. 1999. Mimicry and the judgment of emotional facial expressions. Journal of Nonverbal Behavior. 23 (1): 5-41.

Blum, Miriam D. (1988). The Silent Speech of Politicians (San Diego: Brenner Information Group).

Bohm. 1997. Effects of interpersonal touch, degree of justification, and sex of participant on compliance with a request. The Journal of social psychology. 137: 460-469.

Bond, Michael H., and Hiroshi Komai (1976). "Targets of Gazing and Eye Contact During Interviews: Effects on Japanese Nonverbal Behavior." In Journal of Personality and Social Psychology (Vol. 34), pp. 1276-84.

Bower, Bruce (1992). "Consciousness Raising: Theories Abound Regarding the Vexing Nature of Conscious Experience." In Science News (October 10), pp. 232-35.

Bower, Bruce (1997). "Brain Structure Sounds Off to Fear, Anger." In Science News (Vol. 151, January 18), p. 38.

Boyd, Robert S. (2000). "Scientists Look at How Adult Brains Change." In San Diego Union-Tribune (May 24), p. E-4.

Bradley, Margaret M; Codispoti, Maurizio; Sabatinelli, Dean; Lang, Peter J. 2001. Emotion and motivation II: Sex differences in picture processing Emotion. 1(3): 300-319

Brandt, David R. 1980. A systemic approach to the measurement of dominance in human face-to-face interaction Source: Communication quarterly. 28 (1):31-43.

Brannigan, Christopher, and David Humphries (1969). "I See What You Mean." New Scientist (Vol. 42), pp. 406-08.

Brannigan, Christopher, and David Humphries (1972). "Human Non-Verbal Behaviour, A Means of Communication." In N. G. Blurton-Joned, ed., Ethological Studies of Child Behaviour (Cambridge: University Press), pp. 37-64.

Breed, G., Christiansen, E., & Larson, D. 1972. Effect of lecturer's gaze direction upon teaching effectiveness. Catalog of Selected Documents in Psychology, 2: 115.

Bressler, E.R.; Martin, R.A.; Balshine, S. 2006. Evolution and Human Behavior. Production and appreciation of humor as sexually selected traits. 27 (2):

Bressler, Eric R.; Balshine, Sigal 2006. The influence of humor on desirability. Evolution and Human Behavior. 27(1): 29-39.

Briton, Nancy J.; Hall, Judith A. 1995. Beliefs about female and male nonverbal communication. Sex Roles: A Journal of Research, 32(1): 79-90.

Brockner, J; B. Pressman, J. Cabitt and P. Moran. 1982. Nonverbal intimacy, sex, and compliance: A field study, Journal of Nonverbal Behavior 6: 253–258.

Brody, Robert (1983). "Anatomy of a Laugh." In American Health (November/December), pp. 43-47.

Brooks, C. I., Church, M. A., & Fraser, L. 1986. Effects of duration of eye contact on judgments of personality characteristics. Journal of Social Psychology. 126: 71–78.

Brown, Clifford E.; Dovidio, John F.; Ellyson, Steve L. 1990. Reducing Sex Differences in Visual Displays of Dominance: Knowledge is Power. Personality And Social Psychology Bulletin. 16(2): 358-368.

Bruner, J. (1978). "On Prelinguistic Prerequisites of Speech." In R. N. Campbell and P. T. Smith, eds., Recent Advances in the Psychology of Language (New York: Plenum Press), pp. 199-214.

Buller, D.B., J., Comstock, R.K. Aune, and K.D. Strzyzewski (1989). "The Effects of Probing on Deceivers and Truthtellers." In Journal of Nonverbal Behavior (Vol.13), pp. 189-204.

Burg, A. 1968. Lateral visual field as related to age and sex. Journal of Applied Psychology. 52: 10–15.

206

Burgoon, Judee K., David B. Buller, and W. Gill Woodall (1989). Nonverbal Communication: The

Buss, D. M. 1988. The evolution of human intrasexual competition: tactics of mate attraction. Journal of Personality and Social Psychology 54: 616-628.

Buss, D.M. 1989. Sex differences in human mate preferences: evolutionary hypotheses tested in 37 cultures. Behavioral and Brain Sciences 12: 1-49.

Cahoon, DD; Edmonds, EM 1989. Male-Female Estimates Of Opposite-Sex 1st Impressions Concerning Females Clothing Styles Bulletin of the psychonomic society. 27(3): 280-281.

Calvert, Gemma A., Edward T. Bullmore, Michael J. Brammer, Ruth Campbell, Steven C.R. Williams, Philip K. McGuire, Peter W.R. Woodruff, Susan D. Iversen, and Anthony S. David (1997). "Activation of Auditory Cortex During Silent Lipreading." In Science (Vol. 276, 25 April), pp. 593-96.

Cannon, Walter B. (1929). Bodily Changes in Pain, Hunger, Fear, and Rage, Vol. 2 (New York:

Carlson, Neil R. (1986). Physiology of Behavior, 3rd Edition (Boston: Allyn and Bacon, Inc.).

Carney, Dana R.; Hall, Judith A. LeBeau, Lavonia Smith Beliefs about the nonverbal expression of social power Journal of Nonverbal Behavior. 2005. 29(2):105.

Carroll E. 1994. Innate and universal facial expressions: Evidence from developmental and cross-cultural research Izard, Psychological Bulletin. 115(2): 288-299.

Carter, Rita (1998). Mapping the Mind (Berkeley: University of California Press).

Cashdan, E. 1993. Attracting mates: Effects of paternal investment on mate attraction strategies. Ethology and Sociobiology 14: 1-24.

Caso, L., A. Gnisci, A. Vrij, and S. Mann. 2005. Processes underlying deception: an empirical analysis of truth and lies when manipulating the stakes. Journal of Investigative Psychology and Offender Profiling 2 (3): 195-202.

Chalmers, David J. (1995). "The Puzzle of Conscious Experience." In Scientific American (December), pp. 80-86.

Chaplin William F.; Phillips Jeffrey B; Brown Jonathan D.; Clanton Nancy R.; Stein Jennifer L.; 2000. Handshaking, gender, personality, and first impressions Journal of personality and social psychology. 79(1): 110-117.

Chartrand, T. L., and J. A. Bargh (1999). "The Chameleon Effect: The Perception-Behavior Link and Social Interaction." In Journal of Personality and Social Psycholology (June, Vol. 76, No. 6), pp. 893-910.

Chevalier-Skolnikoff, Suzanne (1973). "Facial Expression of Emotion in Nonhuman Primates." In Paul Ekman, ed., Darwin and Facial Expression (New York: Academic Press), pp. 11-89.

Chowdhary, U. 1988. Instructor's attire as a biasing factor in students' ratings of an instructor. Clothing & Textiles Research Journal 6 (2): 17-22.

Clancy, Susan (2000). "SIS: The Immune System Filtering Friend from Foe." In Signals (a publication of the Salk Institute, La Jolla, Calif., Spring), pp.17-18.

Clements, A. M.; Rimrodt, S. L.; Abel, J. R.; Blankner, J. G.; Mostofsky, S. H.; Pekar, J. J.; Denckla, M. B.; Cutting, L. E. Sex Differences in Cerebral Laterality of Language and Visuospatial Processing. Brain and Language. 2006. 98 (2): 150-158.

Cooper, L. 1976. Mirroring: One vehicle to organizational clarity. International Journal Of Social Psychiatry 22 (4): 288-295.

Coreen Farris; Teresa A. Treat; Richard J. Viken; and Richard M. McFall. 2008. Perceptual Mechanisms That Characterize Gender Differences in Decoding Women's Sexual Intent Psychological Science. 19(4):

Crusco, A. and C. Wetzel. 1984. The midas touch: the effects of interpersonal touch on restaurant tipping, Personality and Social Psychology Bulletin 10: 512–517.

Cuddy, A. J. C., Schultz, S. J., & Fosse, N. E. (2018). P-Curving a More Comprehensive Body of Research on Postural Feedback Reveals Clear Evidential

Cunningham, M. R. 1986. Measuring the physical in physical attractiveness: Quasiexperiments on the sociobiology of female facial beauty. Journal of Personality and Social Psychology, 50: 925–935.

207

Cunningham, M. R., Roberts, A. R., Barbee, A. P., Druen, P. B., & Wu, C. 1995. Consistency and variability in the cross-cultural perception of female physical attractiveness. Journal of Personality and Social Psychology, 68: 261–279.

Damasio, Antonio R. (1994). Descartes' Error: Emotion, Reason, and the Human Brain (New York: G.P.

Daniel, R. 1992. An effect of seating location on course achievement: Comment on Brooks and Rebeta. Environment and Behavior 24(3): 396-399.

Danielle Jackson, Erika Engstrom and Tara Emmers-Sommer. 2007. Think Leader, Think Male and Female: Sex vs. Seating Arrangement as Leadership Cues. Sex Roles. 57 (9/10): 713-723.

Darwin, Charles (1872). The Expression of the Emotions in Man and Animals, third edition (New York:

David Lambert. 2008. Body Language 101. Skyhorse publishing. New York, NY.

Denise Dellarosa Cummins. 1996. Dominance Hierarchies and the Evolution of Human Reasoning. Minds and machines. 6 (4): 463-480.

Davidio, F.M. Brown C.E. Heltman, K. Ellyson, S.L. and Keating, C.F. 1988. Power Displays between Women and Men in Discussion of Gender-linked Tasks: A Multichannel Study, Journal of Personality and Social Psychology 55: 580-7.

Davidson, R. J. & Irwin, W. 1999. The functional neuroanatomy of emotion and affective style. Trends Cogn. Sci. 3: 11–21.

Davis 1978. Camera Eye-Contact by the Candidates in the Presidential Debates of 1976 Source: The journalism quarterly. 55 (3): 431 -437.

Davis, Flora (1971). Inside Intuition: What We Know About Nonverbal Communication (San Francisco:

Davis, S.F., and J.J. Palladino (2000). Psychology (3rd ed.; Upper Saddle River, New Jersey: Prentice-Hall).

Deacon, Terrence (1992). "Primate Brains and Senses." In Steve Jones, Robert Martin and David Pilbeam, Eds. The Cambridge Encyclopedia of Human Evolution. (New York: Cambridge University Press), pp. 109-14.

DePaulo, B. M., & Kashy, D. A. (1998). Everyday lies in close and casual relationships. Journal of Personality and Social Psychology. 74: 63–79.

DePaulo, B. M., J. J. Lindsay, B. E. Malone, L. Muhlenbruck, K. Charlton, and H. Cooper. 2003. Cues to deception. Psychological Bulletin 129: 74-118.

DePaulo, B. M., Kashy, D. A., Kirkendol, S. E., Wyer, M. M., & Epstein, J. A. (1996). Lying in everyday life. Journal of Personality and Social Psychology. 70: 979–995.

Desmond Morris. Peoplewatching: The Desmond Morris Guide to Body Language. Published 2002 by Vintage

D'Esposito, Mark, and Helen Wills (2000). "Functional Imaging of Neurocognition." In Seminars in Neurology (Vol. 20, No. 4), pp. 487-98.

Dilts, R.B., Grinder, J., Bandler, R., & DeLozier, J. 1979. Neuro-linguistic programming L Cupertino, CA: Meta Publications.

Dimitrus, J. and M. Mazzerella. 1998. Reading people: how to understand people and predict their behavior – anytime, anyplace. New York, Random House.

Dindia, K. 1987. The effects of sex of subject and sex of partner on interruptions. Human Communication Research. 13 (3): 345-371.

Doohan, E. 2007. Listening behaviors of married couples: An exploration of nonverbal presentation to a relational outsider. International Journal of Listening, 21 (1): 24-41.

Dovidio JF, Ellyson SL, Keating CF, Heltman K, Brown CE. 1988. The relationship of social power to visual displays of dominance between men and women. Source: Journal of personality and social psychology. 54: 233-42.

Doyle, Arthur Conan (1976). The Complete Adventures and Memoirs of Sherlock Holmes (New York:

Duncan, S. Jr. 1972. Some signals and rules for taking speaking turns in conversation, Journal of Personality and Social Psychology. 23(2): 283-292.

Duncan, W.J., Smeltzer, L.R. & Leap, T.L. Humor and work: Applications of joking behavior to management. Journal of Management, 1990. 16: 255–78.

Eccles, John C. (1995). Evolution of the Brain: Creation of the Self (New York: Routledge).

Edelstein, R. S., T. L. Luten, P. Ekman, and G. S. Goodman. 2006. Detecting lies in children and adults. Law and Human Behavior 30(1): 1-10.

Edmonds, Ed M.; Cahoon, Delwin D.; Hudson, Elizabeth 1992. Male-female estimates of feminine assertiveness related to females' clothing styles. Bulletin of the Psychonomic Society. 30(2): 43-144.

Efron, David (1942). Gesture and Environment (New York: Kings Crown Press).

Efron, David (1972). Gesture, Race and Culture (The Hague: Mouton).

Eibl-Eibesfeldt, I. 1989. Human ethology. Hawthorne, NY: Aldine de Gruyter.

Eibl-Eibesfeldt, Irenaus (1970). Ethology: The Biology of Behavior (San Francisco: Holt, Rinehart, and Winston).

Eibl-Eibesfeldt, Irenaus (1973). "The Expressive Behaviour of the Deaf-and-Blind-Born." In Mario von Cranach and Ian Vine (Eds.), Social Communication and Movement (European Monographs in Social Psychology 4, New York: Academic Press), pp. 163-94.

Ekman, Paul (1984). "Expression and the Nature of Emotion." In K. Scherer and Paul Ekman (Eds.), Approaches to Emotion (Hillsdale, New Hersey: Erlbaum), pp. 319-44.

Ekman, Paul (1992). Telling Lies (New York: W. W. Norton).

Ekman, Paul (1998). Commentaries. In Darwin, Charles (1872). The Expression of the Emotions in Man and Animals, third edition (New York: Oxford University Press, 1998).

Ekman, Paul and Friesen, W. V. 1987. Universals and cultural differences in the judgments of facial expressions of emotion. Journal of Personality and Social Psychology. 53(4): 712-717.

Ekman, Paul, and Wallace V. Friesen (1968). "Nonverbal Behavior in Psychotherapy Research." In John Shlien (Ed.), Research in Psychotherapy (Washington, D.C.: American Psychological Association), pp. 179-216.

Ekman, Paul, and Wallace V. Friesen (1969). "Nonverbal Leakage and Clues to Deception." In Psychiatry (Vol. 32), pp. 88-106.

Ekman, Paul, and Wallace V. Friesen (1969b). "The Repertoire of Nonverbal Behavior: Categories, Origins, Usage, and Coding." In Semiotica (Vol. 1), pp. 49-98.

Ekman, Paul, and Wallace V. Friesen (1971). "Constants Across Cultures in the Face and Emotion." In Journal of Personality and Social Psychology (Vol. 17, No. 2), pp. 124-29.

Ekman, Paul, and Wallace V. Friesen (1972). "Hand Movements." In Journal of Communication (Vol. 22, Dec. 1972), pp. 353-74.

Ekman, Paul, Wallace V. Friesen, and Sylvan S. Tomkins (1971). "Facial Affect Scoring Technique: A First Validity Study." In Semiotica (Vol. 3), pp. 37-58.

Ekman, Paul. 1972. Universals and cultural differences in facial expressions of emotion. In J. Cole (Ed.), Nebraska Symposium on Motivation, 1971. 19: 207-282. Lincoln: University of Nebraska Press.

Ekman, Paul. 1986. A new pan-cultural facial expression of emotion. Source: Motivation and Emotion Ekman. 10(2): 159-168.

Ekman, Paul. 1994. Strong evidence for universals in facial expressions: A reply to Russell's mistaken critique Psychological Bulletin. 115(2): 268-287.

Ekman, Paul. 1996. Why Don't We Catch Liars? 63(3):

Ekman, Paul; Davidson, Richard J and Friesen, Wallace V. 1990. The Duchenne smile: Emotional expression and brain physiology: II . Journal of Personality and Social Psychology. 58(2): 342-353.

Ekman, Paul; Friesen, Wallace V. 1974. Detecting deception from the body or face Journal of Personality and Social Psychology. 29(3): 288-298.

Ekman, Paul; O'Sullivan, Maureen. 1991. Who can catch a liar? American Psychologist. Vol 46(9): 913-920.

Ekman. 1982. Felt, false, and miserable smiles. Journal of nonverbal behavior. 6(4): 238-258.

Elaad, E. 2003. Effects of feedback on the overestimated capacity to detect lies and the underestimated ability to tell lies. Applied Cognitive Psychology 17(3): 349-363.

Eliade, Mircea (1959). The Sacred and the Profane: The Nature of Religion (London: Harcourt Brace Jovanovich).

Elliott, Charles (2001). "Samuel Pepys' London Chronicles." In Smithsonian (July), pp. 102-09.

Ellsworth, Phoebe; Carlsmith, J Merrill. 1973. Eye contact and gaze aversion in an aggressive encounter. Journal of Personality and Social Psychology. 28(2): 280-292.

Engel, George [Prof. of Medicine and Psychiatry, University of Rochester] (1978). "Clinical Value of Gestures, Postures, and Facial Expressions." Public lecture (University of Washington, Seattle, December 5).

Estow, S., J. P. Jamieson, and J. R. Yates. 2007. Self-monitoring and mimicry of positive and negative social behaviors. Journal of Research in Personality 41 (2): 425-433.

Ewer, R. F. (1968). Ethology of Mammals (New York: Plenum).

Fallon, James H., and Philippe Ciofi (1990). "Dynorphin-Containing Neurons." In Björklund, A., T. Hökfelt, and M.J. Kuhar (Eds.), Handbook of Chemical Anatomy (Vol. 9: Neuropeptides in the CNS, Part II; Elsevier Science Publishers B.V.), pp. 1-130.

Fatt, J. P. T. 1998. Nonverbal Communication and Business Success. Management Research News 21(4): 1-10.

Field, T. 2001. Touch. Cambridge, MA: MIT Press.

Fisher, J; Rytting, M and Heslin, R. 1976. Hands touching hands: affective and evaluative effects on interpersonal touch, Sociometry 39: 416–421.

Fisher, Jeffrey, and Donn Byrne (1975). "Too Close for Comfort: Sex Differences in Response to Invasions of Personal Space." In Journal of Personality and Social Psychology (Vol. 32), pp. 15-21.

Foddy, Margaret 1978. Patterns of Gaze in Cooperative and Competitive Negotiation Human Relations. 31(11):925-938.

Forgas. J.P., O'Connor, K.V., and Morris, S.L. 1983. Smile and punishment: The effect of facial expression on responsibility attribution by groups and individuals. Personality and Social Psychology Bulletin, 9: 587-596.

Forsythe, S. M. 1990. Effect of applicant's clothing on interviewer's decision to hire. Journal of Applied Social Psychology 20 (19, 1): 1579-1595.

Forsythe, S., M. F. Drake, and C. E. Cox. 1985. Influence of applicant's dress on interviewer's selection decisions. Journal of Applied Psychology 70 (2): 374-378.

Frank M.G. and Ekman P. 1997. The ability to detect deceit generalizes across different types of high-stake lies. Source: Journal of personality and social psychology. 72: 1429 -39

Frank, M.G; Ekman, P; Friesen, W. V. 1993. Behavior markers and reconcilability of the smile of enjoyment. Journal of personality and social sychology. 64 (1): 83-93.

Friesen, W.V. (1972). Cultural Differences in Facial Expressions in a Social Situation: An Experimental Test of the Concept of Display Rules (University of California, San Francisco, Ph.D. dissertation).

Fugita, Stephen S.; Hogrebe, Mark C.; Wexley, Kenneth N. 1980. Perceptions of Deception: Perceived Expertise in Detecting Deception, Successfulness of Deception and Nonverbal Cues. Personality And Social Psychology Bulletin. 6(4): 637-643.

Fulcher, J. S. "Voluntary" facial expression in blind and seeing children. Archives of Psychology, 1942. 38: 272.

Galin, D. and Ornstein, R., 1974. Individual Differences in Cognitive Style – Reflective Eye Movements; Neuropsychologia, 12: 376-397.

Gallese, V. & Goldman, A., (1998). Mirror neurons and the simulation theory of mind-reading. Trends in Cognitive Sciences. 12: 493-501.

Gangestad, S. W., J. A. Simpson, A. J. Cousins, C. E. Garver-Apgar, and P. N. Christensen. 2004. Women's preferences for male behavioral displays change across the menstrual cycle. Psychological Science 15: 203-207.

Gangestad, S. W., R. Thornhill, and C. E. Garver-Apgar. 2005. Adaptations to ovulation: implications for sexual and social behavior. Current Directions in Psychological Science 14 (6): 312-316.

Gangestad, S.W., Thornhill, R., Garver, C., 2002. Changes in women's sexual interests and their partners' mate retention tactics across the menstrual cycle: Evidence for shifting conflicts of interest. Proc. R. Soc. London, B 269: 975–982.

210

Gangestad, S.W., Thornhill, R., Garver-Apgar, C.E., 2005a. Adaptations to ovulation. In: Buss, D.M. (Ed.), The Handbook of Evolutionary Psychology. John Wiley and Sons, Hoboken, NJ, 344–371.

Gangestad, S.W., Thornhill, R., Garver-Apgar, C.E., 2005b. Women's sexual interests across the ovulatory cycle depend on primary partner fluctuating asymmetry. Proc. R. Soc. London, B 272: 2023-2027.

Gershon, Michael D. (1998). The Second Brain (New York: Harper Collins).

Geschwind, Norman (1979). "Specializations of the Human Brain." In Rodolfo R. Llinás (Ed.), The Workings of the Brain: Development, Memory, and Perception (Readings from Scientific American Magazine, 1976-1987, New York: W. H. Freeman and Co., 1990), pp. 105-20.

Ghez, Claude (1991). "Posture." In Eric R. Kandel, James H. Schwartz and Thomas M. Jessell (Eds.), Principles of Neural Science, 3rd Ed. (Norwalk, Connecticut: Appleton & Lange), Ch. 39, pp. 596-607.

Gilliam, Harold V. B.; Van Den Berg, Sjef. 1980. Different Levels of Eye Contact: Effects on Black and White College Students. Urban Education. 15 (1): 83-92.

Givens, David B. (1976). An Ethological Approach to the Study of Human Nonverbal Communication (University of Washington Ph.D. dissertation in Anthropology, Ann Arbor: University Microfilms).

Givens, David B. (1977B). "Shoulder Shrugging: A Densely Communicative Expressive Behavior." In Semiotica (Vol. 19:1/2), pp. 13-28.

Givens, David B. (1978A). "The Nonverbal Basis of Attraction: Flirtation, Courtship, and Seduction." In Psychiatry (Vol. 41), pp. 346-359.

Givens, David B. (1978D). "Greeting a Stranger: Some Commonly Used Nonverbal Signals of Aversiveness." In Semiotica (Vol. 22), pp. 351-67.

Givens, David B. (1982). "From Here to Eternity: Communicating With the Distant Future." In Et Cetera (Vol. 39, No. 2), pp. 159-79.

Givens, David B. (1983). Love Signals (New York: Crown Publishers).

Givens, David B. (1986). "The Big and the Small: Toward a Paleontology of Gesture." In Sign Language Studies (No. 51, Summer), pp. 145-67.

Glenn E. Weisfeld and Jody M. Beresford. 1982. Erectness of posture as an indicator of dominance or success in humans. Motivation and Emotion. 6(2):113 -131.

Goffman, Erving (1963). Behavior in Public Places (New York: The Free Press).

Goffman, Erving (1967). Interaction Ritual (Chicago: Aldine).

Goldman. 1980. Effect of Eye Contact and Distance on the Verbal Reinforcement of Attitude. The Journal of social psychology 111(1): 73 -78.

Goldstein, Irwin (2000). "Male Sexual Circuitry." In Scientific American (August), pp. 70-5.

Goodall, Jane (1986). The Chimpanzees of Gombe: Patterns of Behavior (Cambridge: Belknap Press of Harvard University).

Gordon, A. K. and A. G. Miller. 2000. Perspective differences in the construal of lies: is deception in the eye of the beholder? Personality and Social Psychology Bulletin 26 (1): 46-55.

Grammer, K., & Eibl-Eibesfeldt, I. 1990. The ritualisation of laughter. In W. Koch (Ed.), Naturalichkeit der Sprache un der Kultur: Acta colloquii 192–214.

Grand, Stanley (1977). "On Hand Movements During Speech: Studies of the Role of Self-Stimulation in Communication Under Conditions of Psychopathology, Sensory Deficit, and Bilingualism." In Norbert Freedman and Stanley Grand, eds., Communicative Structures and Psychic Structures: A Psycholanalytic Interpretation of Communication (New York: Plenum Press), pp. 199-221.

Grant, Ewan (1969). "Human Facial Expressions." In Man (Vol. 4), pp. 525-36.

Graziano, Michael S.A. Cooke, Daylan, F. 2006. Pariieto-frontal Interactions, Personal Space, and Defensive Behavior. Neuropsychologia. 44: 845-59.

Greenberg, J. 1976. The role of seating position in group interaction: a review, with applications for group trainers. Group & Organization Management 1 (3): 310-327.

Greene 1979. Title: Need-Fulfillment and Consistency Theory: Relationships Between Self-Esteem and Eye Contact. Source: Western journal of speech communication. 43(2): 123 -133.

Gregory H. and M. Karinch. 2007. I can read you like a book: how to spot the messages and emotions people are really sending with their body language. Franklin Lakes, Career Press.

Grimshaw, Gina M.; Bulman-Fleming, M. Barbara; Ngo, Cam 2004. A signal-detection analysis of sex differences in the perception of emotional faces. Brain and Cognition. Vol 54(3): 248-250.

Grinder, J., DeLozier, J. and Bandler, R., 1977 Patterns of the Hypnotic Techniques of Milton H. Erickson, M.D. Vol. II

Guéguen, N and C. Jacob 2006, Touch and consumer behavior: A new experimental evidence in a field setting, International Journal of Management 23: 24–33.

Guéguen, N. and C. Jacob, 2005. The Effect of touch on tipping: an evaluation in a French's bar, International Journal of Hospitality Management 24: 295–299.

Gur, Raquel E. (1975). "Conjugate Lateral Eye Movements as an Index of Hemispheric Activation." In Journal of Personality and Social Psychology (Vol. 31), pp. 751-57.

Gurung, R. A. R. and C. J. Chrouser. 2007. Predicting objectification: Do provocative clothing and observer characteristics matter? Sex Roles: A Journal of Research 57 (1-2): 91-99.

Gustafson C. Bruce Lipton, PhD: The Jump From Cell Culture to Consciousness. *Integr Med (Encinitas)*. 2017;16(6):44-50.

Hall, Edward, T. 1959. The silent language. New York: Doubleday.

Hall, Edward, T. The Hidden Dimension, Garden City, NJ: Doubleday, 1966.

Hall, Edward,T. The Silent Language, Greenwich, CT: Fawcett, 1959.

Hall, J. A. 2006.Nonverbal Behavior, Status, and Gender: How Do We Understand Their Relations. Psychology of Women Quarterly; 30(4): 384-391.

Hall. J.A. 1978. Gender effects in decoding nonverbal cues. Psychological Bulletin, 85: 845-857.

Hall. J.A. 1984. Nonverbal sex differences: Communication accuracy and expressive style. Baltimore: The Johns Hopkins University Press.

Hamel, R. F (1974). Female subjective and pupillary reactions to nude male and female figures. Journal of Psychology. 87: 171-175.

Harper, Robert G., Arthur N. Wiens and Joseph D. Matarazzo. Nonverbal communication: The State of the Art. Wiley Series on Personality Processes. New York: John Wiley & Sons, Inc., 1978.

Harrison, Neil A.; Wilson, C. Ellie; Critchley, Hugo D. 2007. Processing of observed pupil size modulates perception of sadness and predicts empathy. Emotion. 7(4): 724-729.

Hasegawa, T. and K. Sakaguchi. 2006. Person perception through gait information and target choice for sexual advances: comparison of likely targets in experiments and real life. Journal of Nonverbal Behavior 30(2): 63-85.

Haselton, M. G., M. Mortezaie, E. G. Pillsworth, A. Bleske-rechek, and D. A. Frederick. 2007. Ovulatory shifts in human female ornamentation: near ovulation, women dress to impress. Hormones and Behavior. 51(1): 40-45.

Hass, Hans (1970). The Human Animal (New York: G.P. Putnam's Sons).

Hatch, M.J. 1997 Irony and the social construction of contradiction in the humor of a management team. Organization Science. 8: 275–88.

Hauser, Marc D. (2000). Wild Minds: What Animals Really Think (New York: Henry Holt and Company).

Haut, Marc W., Hiroto Kuwabara, Sharon Leach, and Robert G. Arias (2000). "Neural Activation During Performance of Number-Letter Sequencing." In Applied Neuropsychology (Vol. 7, No. 4), pp. 237-42.

Havlicek, J., S. C. Roberts, and J. Flegr. 2005. Women's preference for dominant male odour: effects of menstrual cycle and relationship status. Biology Letters 1(3): 256-259.

Hecht, M.A. and LaFrance, M. 1988. License or obligation to smile: The effect of power and gender on amount and type of smiling. Personality and Social Psychology Bulletin, 24: 1326-1336.

Hediger, Heini 1955. Studies of the psychology and behaviour of captive animals in zoos and circuses. Butterworths Scientific Publications

Henle, Paul (1958). "Language, Thought, and Culture." In Peter B.Hammond, ed., Cultural and Social Anthropology (London: Macmillan), pp. 378-92.

Henley, N., 1977. "Body Politics: power, sex and nonverbal communication, prentice hall, new jersey.

Hensley, W. E. 1982. Professor Proxemics: personality and job demands as factors of faculty office arrangement. Environment and Behavior 14(5): 581-591.

Henss, Ronald. (2000). "Waist-to-Hip Ratio and Female Attractiveness: Evidence from Photographic Stimuli and Methodological Considerations." In Personality and Individual Differences (Vol. 28), pp. 501-13.

Hermans, E. J., P. Putman, and J. van Honk. 2006. Testosterone administration reduces empathetic behavior: a facial mimicry study. Psychoneuroendocrinology 31(7): 859-866.

Hertenstein, Matthew J; Keltner, Dacher; App, Betsy; Bulleit, Brittany A; Jaskolka, Ariane R 2006. Touch Communicates Distinct Emotions. Emotion. 6(3): 528-533

Hess, E. H. (1975). "The Role of Pupil Size in Communication." In Scientific American (Vol. 233), pp.

Hess, E. H. 1965. Attitude and pupil size. Scientific American, 212 (4): 46–54.

Hess, E. H. 1975. The role of pupil size in communication. Scientific American. 233(5): 110–119.

Hess, E. H., & Polt, J. M. (1960). Pupil size as related to the interest value of visual stimuli. Science, 132: 349-350.

Hewes, Gordon (1957). "The Anthropology of Posture." In Scientific American (Vol. 196), pp. 122-32.

Hill, Jane H. (1977). "Apes, Wolves, Birds, and Humans: Toward a Comparative Foundation for a Functional Theory of Language Evolution." In Sign Language Studies (14), pp. 21-58.

Hocking. 1985. Eye contact contrast effects in the employment interview. Communication research reports 2(1): 5-10.

Hockstader, Lee (1992). "Europeans, Latins Split on Bananas." In Washington Post (July 1).

Holdaway, S. Blue jokes: Humour in police work. In C. Powell & G.E.C. Paton (Eds), Humour in society: Resistance and control. Houndsmills: Macmillan, 1988, 106–22.

Hopson, Janet (1980). "Growl, Bark, Whine & Hiss: Deciphering the Common Elements of Animal Language." In Science 80 (May/June), pp. 81-4.

Hornik, J 1992. Tactile stimulation and consumer response, Journal of Consumer Research 19: 449–458.

Howells, L. T. and S. W. Becker. 1962. Seating arrangement and leadership emergence.The Journal of Abnormal and Social Psychology 64(2): 148-150.

Irwin Silverman, Jean Choi, and Michael Peters. 2007. The hunter-gatherer theory of sex differences in spatial abilities: Data from 40 countries. Archives of Sexual Behavior. 36 (2): 261-268.

Isaacson, Robert L. (1974). The Limbic System (New York: Plenum Press).

Izard, Carroll E. (1971). The Face of Emotion (New York: Appleton-Century-Crofts).

James A. Coan; Hillary S, Schaefer; and Richard J. Davidson. 2006. Lending a Hand. Social Regulation of the Neural Response to Threat. Association for Psychological Science

Janisse, Michel Pierre. 1973. Pupil Size and Affect: A Critical Review of the Literature Since 1960. Canadian Psychologist Psychologie Canadienne. 14(4): 311-329.

Jansen, Arthur S. P., Xay Van Nguyen, Vladimir Karpitskiy, Thomas C. Mettenleiter, and Arthur D. Loewy (1995). "Central Command Neurons of the Sympathetic Nervous System: Basis of the Fight-or-Flight Response." In Science (Vol. 270, 27 October), pp. 644-46.

Jeffrey D. Fisher; Marvin Rytting; Richard Heslin. 1976. Hands Touching Hands: Affective and Evaluative Effects of an Interpersonal Touch. Sociometry, 39(4): 416-421.

Jerison, Harry J. (1976). "Paleoneurology and the Evolution of Mind." In Rodolfo R. Llinás, ed., The Workings of the Brain: Development, Memory, and Perception (Readings from Scientific American Magazine, 1976-1987, New York: W. H. Freeman and Co., 1990), pp. 3-16.

Joe Navarro. 2008. What Every BODY is Saying: An Ex-FBI Agent's Guide to Speed-Reading People. William Morrow Paperbacks.

213

John F. Dpvidio, Karen Heltman, Clifford E. Brown, Steve L. Ellyson, Caroline F. Keating. 1988. Power Displays Between Women and Men in Discussions of Gender-

Johnsen, Sönke (2000). "Transparent Animals." In Scientific American (February), pp. 80-88.

Joseph, R. 2000. The evolution of sex differences in language, sexuality, and visual-spatial skills. Archives of Sexual Behavior. 29(1): 35-66.

Julius F. 1977. The body language of sex, power, and aggression. New York, M. Evans and Company Inc.

Kandel, Eric R. (1979). "Small Systems of Neurons." In Rodolfo R. Llinás (ed.), The Biology of the Brain: From Neurons to Networks (Chapter 5, Readings from Scientific American Magazine, 1977-1988, New York: W. H. Freeman and Co.), pp. 70-86.

Kandel, Eric R., James H. Schwartz, and Thomas M. Jessell, eds. (1991). Principles of Neural Science, 3rd Ed. (Norwalk, Connecticut: Appleton & Lange).

Kandel, James H. Schwartz and Thomas M. Jessell (Eds.), Principles of Neural Science, 3rd Ed.

Kanfer, F. (1960). "Verbal Rate, Eyeblink, and Content in Structured Psychiatric Interviews." In Journal of Abnormal and Social Psychology (Vol. 61, No. 3), pp. 341-47.

Kansaku, K., & Kitazawa, S. 2001. Imaging studies on sex divergences in the lateralization of language. Neuroscience Research. 41: 333–337.

Kaufman, D. and J. Mahoney. 1999 The effect of waitresses' touch on alcohol consumption in dyads, The Journal of Social Psychology 139: 261–267.

Kellerman. 1989. Looking and loving: The effects of mutual gaze on feelings of romantic love. Journal of Research in Personality. 23(2): 145-161.

Kelly, James P., and Jane Dodd (1991). "Anatomical Organization of the Nervous System." In Eric R.

Keltner, D., Ekman, P., 2003. Expression of emotion. In: Davidson, R., Scherer, K., Goldsmith, H. (Eds.), Handbook of Affective Sciences. Oxford University Press, New York, 411–414.

Kendon, A. 1994. Do gestures communicate? A review. Research on Language and Social Intraction. 27(3): 175-200.

Kendon, A. Some Functions of Gaze Direction in Social Interaction. Acta Psychologica. 1967. 32: 1-25.

Kendon, Adam (1967). "Some Functions of Gaze-Direction in Social Interaction." In Acta Psychologica (Vol. 26), pp. 22-63.

Kenner, Andrew N. (1993). "A Cross-Cultural Study of Body-Focused Hand Movement." In Journal of Nonverbal Behavior (Vol. 17, No. 4, Winter), pp. 263-79.

Kiehl, K.A., P.F. Liddle, et al. (1999). "Neural Pathways Involved in the Processing of Concrete and Abstract Words." In Human Brain Mapping (Vol. 7, No. 4), pp. 225-233.

Killackey, Herbert P. (1995). "Evolution of the Human Brain: A Neuroanatomical Perspective." In

Kim, J.J., N.C. Andreasen, et al. (1999). "Direct Comparison of the Neural Substrates of Recognition Memory for Words and Faces." In Brain (Vol. 122, No. 6), pp. 1069-83.

Kimble, Daniel P. (1988). Biological Psychology (New York: Holt, Rinehart and Winston, Inc.).

Kleinke, C. L. 1980. Interaction between gaze and legitimacy of request on compliance in a field setting. Journal of Nonverbal Behavior 5(1): 3-12.

Knackstedt, G., & Kleinke, C. L. (1991). Eye contact, gender, and personality judgments. Journal of Social Psychology, 131: 303-304.

Knapp, Mark L. (1972). Nonverbal Communication in Human Interaction (New York: Holt, Rinehart and Winston).

Knapp, Mark. Nonverbal Communication in Human Interaction, New York: Holt, Rinehart & Winston, 1992.

Kocel, K., et al.,1972. Lateral Eye Movement and Cognitive Mode; Psychon Sci. 27: 223-224.

Konopacki 1987. Eye Movement Betrays a Prospect's Inner Feelings Source: Marketing news 21(10): 4.

214

Krumhuber, E ; Manstead, A.S.R; Kappas, A. 2007. Temporal Aspects of Facial Displays in Person and Expression Perception: The Effects of Smile Dynamics, Head-tilt, and Gender. Journal of Nonverbal Behavior. 31: 39-56.

Krumhuber, E., & Kappas, A. (2005). Moving smiles: The role of dynamic components for the perception of the genuineness of smiles. Journal of Nonverbal Behavior. 29: 3-24.

LaBarre, Weston (1947). "The Cultural Basis of Emotions and Gestures." In Journal of Personality (Vol.16), pp. 49-68.

LaFrance, Marianne 1996. Why do women smile more than men? International Journal of Psychology. 31(3-4): 5042-5042.

LaFrance, Marianne, Hecht, M.A., & Levy Paluck, E 2003. The contingent smile: A meta-analysis of sex differences in smiling. Psychological Bulletin, 129: 305-334.

LaFrance, Marianne. 1979. Nonverbal synchrony and rapport: analysis by the cross-lag panel technique. Social Psychology Quarterly 42: 66-70.

LaFrance, Marianne. 1982. Posture mirroring and rapport. In M. Davis (Ed.) Interaction rhythms: periodicity in communicative behavior (279-298). New York, Human Sciences Press, Inc.

LaFrance, Marianne. 1995. Why smiles generate leniency?; Hecht, Marvin A Personality and Social Psychology Bulletin, 21: 207-14.

LaFrance, Marianne. 2003. The Contingent Smile: A Meta-Analysis of Sex Differences in Smiling Source: Psychological bulletin. 129(2):305-334.

LaFrance, Marianne. and W. Ickes. 1981. Posture mirroring and interactional involvement: sex and sex typing effects. Journal of Nonverbal Behavior 5: 139-154.

Lakin, J. L. 2003. The chameleon effect as social glue: evidence for the evolutionary significance of non-conscious mimicry. Journal of Nonverbal Behavior 27 (3): 145-162.

Lakin, J. L., and T. L. Chartrand. 2003. Using non-conscious behavioral mimicry to create affiliation and rapport. Psychological Science 14 (4): 334-339.

LeDoux, Joseph (1996). The Emotional Brain: The Mysterious Underpinnings of Emotional Life (NewYork: Simon & Schuster).

Leroi-Gourhan, André (1964). Gesture and Speech (Cambridge: MIT Press, 1993).

LeVay, Simon (1993). The Sexual Brain (Cambridge: MIT Press).

Leventhal, G. 1978, Sex and setting effects on seating arrangement. Journal of Psychology. 100: 21-26.

Levine, D. W., E. C. O'neal, S. G. Garwood, and P. J. Mcdonald. 1980. Classroom ecology: the effects of seating position on grades and participation. Personality and Social Psychology Bulletin 6 (3): 409-412.

Lewis, David. 1999. The Secret Language Of Success. BBS Publishing Corporation.

Lieberman, Joel D.; Sales, Bruce D. 2007. In-Court Observations of Nonverbal Behavior. Scientific jury selection. (pp. 125-142). Washington, DC, US: American Psychological Association. ix, 261 pp.

Linden, Eugene (1992). "Apes and Humans, A Curious Kinship." In National Geographic (March), pp. 2-53.

Littlepage, Glenn E.; Whiteside, Harold D. 1983. The "Peripheral Cue Shift" Phenomenon: Influence of Facial Expression and Level of Commission on Attribution of Responsibility Personality And Social Psychology Bulletin, 9(2): 261-265.

Lott, D. F. and R. Sommer. 1967. Seating arrangements and status. Journal of Personality and Social Psychology 7 (1): 90-95.

Lurie, Alison. The Language of Clothes. (New York, 1981), 3-26.

MacLean, Paul D. (1967). "The Brain in Relation to Empathy and Medical Education." In Journal of Nervous and Mental Disease (Vol. 144), pp. 374-82).

MacLean, Paul D. (1973). A Triune Concept of the Brain and Behaviour (Toronto: University of Toronto Press).

MacLean, Paul D. (1975). "Sensory and Perceptive Factors in Emotional Functions of the Triune Brain." In L. Levi, ed., Emotions: Their Parameters and Measurement (New York: Raven Publishers), pp. 71-92.

MacLean, Paul D. (1990). The Triune Brain in Evolution (New York: Plenum Press).

Maddux, W. W., E. Mullen, and A. D. Galinsky. 2008. Chameleons bake bigger pies and take bigger pieces: strategic behavioral mimicry facilitates negotiation outcomes. Journal of Experimental Social Psychology 44(2): 461-468.

Mahl, George (1968). "Gestures and Body Movements in Interviews." In John Shlien (Ed.), Research in Psychotherapy (Washington, D.C.: American Psychological Association), pp. 295-346.

Maisey, D. S. (1999). "Characteristics of Male Attractiveness for Women." In Lancet (May 1, 1999).

Mann, S., A. Vrij, and R. Bull. 2002. Suspects, lies, and videotape: an analysis of authentic high-stake liars. Law and Human Behavior 26 (3): 365-376.

Mann, S., A. Vrij, and R. Bull. 2004. Detecting true lies: police officers' ability to detect suspects' lies. Journal of Applied Psychology 89(1): 137-149.

Manstead, A. and A. Kappas. 2007. Temporal aspects of facial displays in person and expression perception: the effects of smile dynamics, head-tilt, and gender. Journal of Nonverbal Behavior 31(1): 39-56.

Matsumoto. 1987. Cultural similarities and differences in the semantic dimensions of body postures. Source: Journal of nonverbal behavior. 11(3):166-179.

Mayes, Andrew (1979). "The Physiology of Fear and Anxiety." In W. Sluckin (Ed.), Fear in Animals and Man (New York: Van Nostrand Reinhold), pp. 24-55.

Mazur, Allan, and Ulrich Mueller (1996). "Facial Dominance." In A. Somit and S. Peterson (Eds.), Research in Biopolitics (Vol. 4, London: JAI Press), pp. 99-111.

McAndrew. 1986. Arousal seeking and the maintenance of mutual gaze in same and mixed sex dyads Source: Journal of nonverbal behavior. 10(3):168-172.

McBride, Glen, M. G. King, and J. W. James (1965). "Social Proximity Effects on GSR in Adult Humans." In Journal of Psychology (Vol. 61), pp. 153-57.

McCall, William (2000). "Staying a Step Ahead." In Spokesman-Review (November 25), p. A14.

McCaskey, M. B. 1979. The hidden messages managers send. Harvard Business Review, Boston. 57 (6): 135.

McClure, E.B. 2000. A meta- analytic review of sex differences in facial expression processing and their development in infants, children, and adolescents. Psychological Bulletin. 126: 424-453.

McClure, Erin B 2000. A meta-analytic review of sex differences in facial expression processing and their development in infants, children, and adolescents Psychological Bulletin. 126(3): 424-453.

McElroy, J. C., P. C. Morrow, and R. J. Ackerman. 1983. Personality and interior office design: exploring the accuracy of visitor attributions. Journal of Applied Psychology. 68 (3): 541-544.

McGhee, Paul E. 1984 Current American Psychological Research on Humor. Jahrbuche fur Internationale Germanistik 16(2): 37-57.

Mcguire, Michael T. 1982. Social Dominance Relationships in Male Vervet Monkeys: A Possible Model for the Study of Dominance Relationships in Human Political Systems. International Political Science Review. 3(1): 11-32.

Mead, M. 1975. Review of "Darwin and facial expression." Journal of Communication, 25: 209-213.

Mealey, L., R. Bridgstock, and G. C. Townsend (1999). "Symmetry and Perceived Facial Attractiveness: A Monozygotic Co-twin Comparison." In Journal of Personality and Social Psycholology (January, Vol. 76, No. 1), pp.151-58.

Mehrabian, A., Friar, J., 1969. Encoding of attitude by a seated communicator via posture and position cues. Journal of Consulting and Clinical Psychology 33: 330–336.

Mehrabian, Albert (1969). "Significance of Posture and Position in the Communication of Attitude and Status Relationships." In Psychological Bulletin (Vol. 71), pp. 359-72.

Mehrabian, Albert (1972). Nonverbal Communication (Chicago: Aldine).

216

Mehrabian, Albert (1974). "Communication Without Words." In Jean Civikly, ed., Messages: A Reader

Meisner, Jane S. (1998). "Emotional Intelligence." In Better Homes and Gardens (May), pp. 102, 104, 106.

Mesquita, B., 2003. Emotions as dynamic cultural phenomena. In: Davidson, R., Scherer, K., Goldsmith, H. (Eds.), Handbook of Affective Sciences. Oxford University Press, New York, 871–890.

Michael S. Gazzaniga (Ed.), The Cognitive Neurosciences (Ch. 82; Cambridge: MIT Press), pp. 1243-53.

Michelini, RL, Passalacqua, R., & Cusimano, J. 1976. Effects of seating arrangement on group participation. Journal of Social Psychology. 99: 179-186.

Middlemist, R. D., E. S. Knowles, and C. F. Matter. 1976. Personal space invasions in the lavatory: suggestive evidence for arousal. Journal of Personality and Social Psychology 33(5): 541-546.

Miles, L. and V. Peace. 2006. Implicit behavioral mimicry: investigating the impact of group membership. Journal of Nonverbal Behavior 30(3): 97-113.

Milgram, Stanley (1974). Obedience to Authority: An Experimental View (London: Tavistock).

Mobbs, N.A. 1968. Eye-contact in Relation to Social Introversion-Extraversion. British Journal of Social Clinical Psychology 7: 305-306.

Molloy, John T. (1988). John T. Molloy's New Dress for Success (New York: Warner Books).

Montello, D. R. 1988. Classroom seating location and its effect on course achievement, participation, and attitudes. Journal of Environmental Psychology 8(2): 149-157.

Moody, E. J., D. N. McIntosh, L. J. Mann, and K. R. Weisser. 2007. More than mere mimicry? The influence of emotion on rapid facial reactions to faces. Emotion. 7(2): 447-457.

Moore, M. M. 1985. Nonverbal courtship patterns in women: context and consequences. Ethology and Sociobiology 64: 237-247.

Moore, M. M. 2001. Flirting. In C. G. Waugh (Ed.) Let's talk: A cognitive skills approach to interpersonal communication. Newark, Kendall-Hunt.

Moore, M. M. and D. L. Butler. 1989. Predictive aspects of nonverbal courtship behavior in women. Semiotica 76(3/4): 205-215.

Morris, Charles (1946). Signs, Language and Behavior (New York: Prentice-Hall).

Morris, Desmond (1977). Manwatching: A Field-Guide to Human Behaviour (London: Jonathan Cape).

Morris, Desmond (1994). Bodytalk: The Meaning of Human Gestures (New York: Crown Publishers).

Morris, Desmond. Peoplewatching. London: Vintage, 2002.

Morris, Jan (1974). Conundrum: From James to Jan--An Extraordinary Personal Narrative of Morris, Ramona, and Desmond Morris (1966). Men and Apes (London: Hutchinson).

Morris, T. L., J. Gorham, S. H. Cohen, and D. Huffman. 1996. Fashion in the classroom: effects of attire on student perceptions of instructors in college classes. Communication Education 45(2): 135.

Morrison, K., M. Ferrara, H. S. Park, T. R. Levine, and S. A. McCornack. 2002. How people really detect lies. Communication Monographs 69(2): 144.

Morrow, P. C. and J. C. McElroy. 1981. Interior office design and visitor response: a constructive replication. Journal of Applied Psychology 66(5): 646-650.

Morsbach, H. (1973). "Aspects of Nonverbal Communication in Japan." In Journal of Nervous and Mental Disease (Vol. 157), pp. 262-77.

Mulac, A., Studley, L., Wiemann, J., & Bradac, J. 1987. Male/female gaze in same-sex and mixed-sex dyads. Human Communication Research. 13: 323-343.

Murphy, Robert F. (1987). The Body Silent (New York: Henry Holt and Co.).

Nakamura, K., R. Kawashima, et al. (1999). "Activation of the Right Inferior Frontal Cortex During Assessment of Facial Emotion." In Journal of Neurophysiology (Vol. 82, No. 3), pp. 1610-14.

Natale, Michael. 1976. A Markovian model of adult gaze behavior. Journal of Psycholinguistic Research. 5(1): 53-63.

Nathan, Peter (1988). The Nervous System (3rd Edition, New York: Oxford University Press).

Nauta, Walle J. H. and Michael Feirtag (1979). "The Organization of the Brain." In Rodolfo R. Llinás (Ed.), The Workings of the Brain: Development, Memory, and Perception (Readings from Scientific American Magazine, 1976-1987, New York: W. H. Freeman and Co., 1990), pp. 17-36.

Nierenberg, G.I. 1983. Negotiating Strategies and Counterstrategies: How to Develop Win/Win Techniques. Management Review, 72: 48-49.

Nierenberg, Gerald, and Henry Calero (1973). How to Read a Person Like a Book (New York: Pocket Books).

Norton, R. (1983). Communicator Style: Theory, Applications, and Measures (Beverly Hills: Sage Publications).

Norum, G. A., N. J. Russo, and R. Sommer. 1967. Seating patterns and group tasks. Psychology in the Schools 4(3): 276-280.

Norum, G.A., Russo, N.J., and Sommer, R. 1967. Seating patterns and group tasks. Source: Psychology in the schools. 4(3): 276-280.

Owren, Michael J.; Bachorowski, Jo-Anne 2003. Reconsidering the evolution of nonlinguistic communication: the case of laughter Journal of Nonverbal Behavior. 27(3): 183-200.

Panksepp, J. 1998. Affective Neuroscience: The Foundation of Human and Animal Emotions. Oxford Univ. Press, New York.

Park, H. S., T. R. Levine, S. A. McCornack, K. Morrison, and M. Ferrara. 2002. How people really detect lies. Communication Monographs. 69: 144-157.

Parrill, F. and I. Kimbara. 2006. Seeing and hearing double: the influence of mimicry in speech and gesture on observers. Journal of Nonverbal Behavior 30(4): 157-166.

Pascual-Leone A, Nguyet D, Cohen LG, Brasil-Neto JP, Cammarota A, Hallett M. Modulation of muscle responses evoked by transcranial magnetic stimulation during the acquisition of new fine motor skills. J Neurophysiol. 1995 Sep;74(3):1037-45. doi: 10.1152/jn.1995.74.3.1037. PMID: 7500130.

Patrington. 1997. NLP for Business Success: How to Master Neuro-Linguistic Programming. Management Research News. 20(8): 43.

Patterson, Miles L.; Montepare, Joann M. 2007. Nonverbal behavior in a global context dialogue questions and responses. Journal of Nonverbal Behavior. 31(3): 167-168.

Pease, Barbara and Allan Pease. 2006. The Definitive Book of Body Language Hardcover. Bantam.

Peluchette, J. V., K. Karl, and K. Rust. 2006. Dressing to impress: beliefs and attitudes regarding workplace attire. Journal of Business and Psychology 21(1): 45-63.

Penton-Voak, I. S., D. I. Perrett, D. Castles, M. Burt, T. Kobayashi, and L. K. Murray. 1999. Female preference for male faces changes cyclically. Nature 399: 741-742.

Peterson, Robin T. 2005. An Examination of the Relative Effectiveness of Training in Nonverbal Communication: Personal Selling Implications. Journal of Marketing Education. 27(2): 143-150.

Pike, Kenneth (1956). "Towards a Theory of the Structure of Human Behavior." In Ruth Brend, ed., Kenneth Pike: Selected Writings (The Hague: Mouton, 1972), pp. 106-16.

Pillsworth, E. G., M. G. Haselton and D. M. Buss. 2004. Ovulatory shifts in female sexual desire. Journal of Sex Research. 41: 55-65.

Prkachin, Kenneth M., and Kenneth D. Craig (1995). "Expressing Pain: The Communication and Interpretation of Facial Pain Signals." In Journal of Nonverbal Behavior (Vol. 19, No. 4, Winter), pp. 191-205.

Provine, R.R. Contagious yawning and laughing: Everyday imitation and mirror-like behavior. Behavioral and Brain Science. 28: 142.

Provine, Robert R. (1996). "Laughter." In American Scientist (Web document, January-February).

Puts, D.A. 2005. Mating context and menstrual phase affect women's preference for male voice pitch. Evolution and Human Behavior 26: 388-397.

218

Puts, D.A. 2007. Men's voices as dominance signals: Vocal fundamental and formant frequencies influence dominance attributions among men. Source: Evolution and human behavior 28(5): 340-344.

Quiatt, Duane, and Vernon Reynolds (1993). Primate Behaviour: Information, Social Knowledge, and the Evolution of Culture (Cambridge, Cambridge University Press).

Quilliam, Susan. 2004. Body Language: Learn to read and use the body's secrete signals. Firefly books Inc.

R. Stephen and R. Zweigenhaft. 1986. The effect on tipping of a waitress touching male and female customers. The Journal of Social Psychology 126 pp. 141–142.

Raffler-Engel, Walburga von (1984). "The Coordination of Verbal and Nonverbal Interaction Towards Three Parties: The Analysis of a Talk Show." Linguistic Agency, University of Trier (Series B., Paper No. 109, July).

Raloff, J. (1995). "Languishing Languages: Cultures at Risk." In Science News (February 25), p. 117.

Ramsey, S.J. (1983). "Double Vision: Nonverbal Behavior East and West." Paper presented at Second International Conference on Nonverbal Behavior (Toronto).

Rasch, Philip J. (1978). Kinesiology and Applied Anatomy (U.S.A.: Lea & Febiger).Richmond, Virginia P., James C. McCroskey and Steven K. Payne (1991). Nonverbal Behavior in Interpersonal Relations (2nd Ed., Englewood Cliffs, New Jersey: Prentice Hall).

Remland, M. S. and T. S. Jones 1995. Interpersonal Distance, Body Orientation, and Touch: Effects of Culture, Gender, and Age. Journal of Social Psychology 135(3): 281-297.

Richard Tessler and Lisa Sushelsky. 1978. Effects of eye contact and social status on the perception of a job applicant in an employment interviewing situation. Journal of Vocational Behavior 13(3): 338-347.

Riess, M. and P. Rosenfeld. 1980. Seating preferences as nonverbal communication: a self-presentational analysis. Journal of Applied Communications Research 8(1): 22.

Rogers, W. T. and S. E. Jones. 1975. Effects of dominance tendencies on floor holding and interruption behavior in dyadic interaction. Human Communication Research I: 113-122.

Rosenfeld, H., Breck, B., Smith, S., & Kehoe, S. 1984. Intimacy-mediators of the proximity-gaze compensation effect: Movement, conversational role, acquaintance, and gender. Journal of Nonverbal Behavior. 8: 235-249.

Rosenfeld, Howard (1973). "Nonverbal Reciprocation of Approval: An Experimental Analysis." In Argyle *, pp. 163-72.

Rosenthal, Robert, and Bella M. DePaulo (1979). "Sex Differences in Accommodation in Nonverbal Communication." In Robert Rosenthal, ed., Skill in Nonverbal Communication (Cambridge, Mass.: Gunn & Hain), pp. 68-103.

Rozin P., L. Lowery, and R. Ebert (1994). "Varieties of Disgust Faces and the Structure of Disgust." In Journal of Personality and Social Scholrolology (Vol. 66, No. 5, May), pp. 870-81.

Rubinstein, Ruth P. (1994). Dress Codes: Meanings and Messages in American Culture.

Ruch, Willibald (1993). "Exhilaration and Humor." In M. Lewis and J. M. Haviland, eds., The Handbook of Emotion (Ch. 42; New York: Guilford Publications), pp. 605-16.

Ruch, Willibald, and Paul Ekman 2001. "The Expressive Pattern of Laughter." In A.W. Kaszniak, ed., Emotion, Qualia, and Consciousness (Tokyo: Word Scientific Publisher), pp. 426-43Russell, P. A. (1979). "Fear-Evoking Stimuli." In W. Sluckin, ed., Fear in Animals and Man (London:

Russell, James A. 1994. Is There Universal Recognition of Emotion From Facial Expression? A Review of the Cross-Cultural Studies. Psychological Bulletin. 115(1): 102-141.

Russell, James A. 1995. Facial Expressions of Emotion: What Lies Beyond Minimal Universality? Psychological bulletin. 118(3): 379-391.

Rutter, D.C; D. C. Pennington, M. E. Dewey and J. Swain. 1984. Eye-contact as a chance product of individual looking: Implications for the intimacy model of Argyle and Dean. Source: Journal of nonverbal behavior. 8(4): 250-258.

Sapir, Edward (1927). "The Unconscious Patterning of Behavior in Society." In David Mandelbaum, ed., Selected Writings of Edward Sapir (Los Angeles: University of California Press, 1958), pp. 544-59.

Sapir, Edward (1931). "Communication." In David Mandelbaum, ed., Selected Writings of Edward Sapir (Los Angeles: University of California Press, 1958), pp. 104-09.

Sato, W. and S. Yoshikawa. 2007. Spontaneous facial mimicry in response to dynamic facial expressions. Cognition 104(1): 1-18

Scalaidhe, Seamas P.O., Fraser A.W. Wilson, and Patricia S. Goldman-Rakic (1997). "Areal Segregation of Face-Processing Neurons in Prefontal Cortex." In Science (November 7, Vol. 278), p. 1135.

Schacter, Daniel L. (1996). Searching for Memory: The Brain, The Mind, and the Past (New York:

Scharlemann, Jorn P. W., Eckel, Catherine C., Kacelnik, Alex, Wilson, Rick K. 2001. The value of a smile: Game theory with a human face. Journal of Economic Psychology. 22(5): 617-640.

Scheflen, Albert (1972). Body Language and the Social Order (New Jersey: Prentice-Hall).

Scheflen, Albert (1973). How Behavior Means (New York: Gordon and Breach).

Scherer, K.R., Wallbott, H.G., Matsumoto, D., Kudoh, T., 1988. Emotional experience in cultural context: a comparison between Europe, Japan, and the United states. In: Scherer, K.R. (Ed.), Faces of Emotions. Erlbaum, Hillsdale, NJ.

Schleidt, 1980. Personal odor and nonverbal communication. Ethology and Sociobiology. 1(3): 225-231.

Sergent J., S. Ohta, and B. MacDonald (1992). "Functional Neuroanatomy of Face and Object Processing." In Brain (Vol. 115), pp. 15-36.

Shaywitz, Bennett A. et al. (1995). "Sex Differences in the Functional Organization of the brain for Language." In Nature (Vol. 373, 16 February), pp. 607-09).

Sherzer, Joel (1973). "Nonverbal and Verbal Deixis: The Pointed Lip Gesture Among the San Blas Cuna." In Language in Society (Vol. 2, No. 1), pp. 117-31.

Silverman, I., & Eals, M. 1992. Sex differences in spatial abilities: Evolutionary theory and data. In J. H. Barkow, L. Cosmides, & J. Tooby (Eds.), The adapted mind: Evolutionary psychology and the generation of culture (pp. 531–549). New York: Oxford Press.

Simone, Pika; Nicoladis, Elena; Marentette, Paula, F. A cross-cultural study on the use of gestures: Evidence for cross-linguistic transfer? Bilingualism Language and Cognition. 9(3): 319 -327

Simons, D.J., and Chabris, C.F. 1999. Gorillas in our midst: Sustained inattentional blindness for dynamic events. Perception 28: 1059-1074.

Sitton, Sarah C; Griffin, Susan T. 1981. Detection of deception from clients' eye contact patterns. Journal of Counseling Psychology. 28(3): 269-271.

Skinner. 2003. Speaking the same language: the relevance of neuro-linguistic programming to effective marketing communications Source: Journal of Marketing Communications. 9(3): 177-192.

Smith, D. E., Gier, J. A., & Willis, F. N. 1982. Interpersonal touch and compliance with a marketing request. Basic and Applied Social Psychology. 3: 35-38.

Smith, John, Julia Chase, and Anna Lieblich (1974). "Tongue Showing." In Semiotica (Vol. 11, No. 3), pp. 201-46.

Snyder, Lynn S. (1978). "Communicative and Cognitive Abilities and Disabilities in the Sensorimotor Period." In Merrill-Palmer Quarterly (Vol. 24), pp. 161-80.

Sommer, R. 1959. Studies in personal space. Sociometry 22: 247-260.

Sommer, R. 1965. Further studies of small group ecology. Sociometry 28: 337-348.

Sommer, R. 1967. Classroom ecology. The Journal Of Applied Behavioral Science 3(4): 489-503.

Sommer, R. 1967. Socifugal space. American Journal of Sociology 72(6): 654-659.

Sommer, Robert (1967). "Small Group Ecology." In Psychological Bulletin (Vol. 67, No. 2), pp. 145-52.

Sommer, Robert (1969). Personal Space: The Behavioral Basis of Design (Englewood Cliffs, New Jersey: Prentice-Hall).

Spinney, Laura (2000). "Bodytalk." In New Scientist (April 8).

Sporer, S. L. and B. Schwandt. 2007. Moderators of nonverbal indicators of deception: A meta-analytic synthesis. Psychology, Public Policy, and Law 13: 1-34.

Starkey, Duncan, and Donald W. Fiske (1977). Face-to-Face Interaction: Research, Methods, and Theory (New York, John Wiley).

Stephen, Jolly. 2000. Understanding body language: Birdwhistell's theory of kinesics Corporate communications. 5(3): 133-139.

Stephenson, G. M. and B. K. Kniveton. 1978. Interpersonal and interparty exchange: an experimental study of the effect of seating position on the outcome of negotiations between teams representing parties in dispute. Human Relations 31(6): 555-566.

Stern, Daniel and Estelle Bender (1974). "An Ethological Study of Children Approaching a Strange Adult." In Richard Friedman et al. (Eds.), Sex Differences in Behavior (New York: John Wiley and Sons), pp. 233-58.

Stokoe, William C. (1986). "Where Should We Look for Language?" In Sign Language Studies (No. 51, Summer), pp. 171-81.(May17), pp.

Street-Smart Executive (New York: Bantam Books).

Stromwell, L. A., P. A. Granhag, and S. Landstrom. 2007. Children's prepared and unprepared lies: can adults see through their strategies? Applied Cognitive Psychology 21 (4): 457-471.

Thornhill, R. and S. W. Gangestad. 1999. The scent of symmetry: a human pheromone that signals fitness? Evolution and Human Behavior 20: 175-201.

Thornhill, R., S. W. Gangestad, R. Miller, G. Scheyd, J. McCollough, and M. Franklin. 2003. MHC, symmetry and body scent attractiveness in men and women (Homo sapiens). Behavioral Ecology 14: 668-678.

Tombs, Selina; Silverman, Irwin 2004. Pupillometry: A sexual selection approach. Evolution and Human Behavior. 25(4): 221-228.

Tracy, Jessica L; Robins, Richard W 2008. The nonverbal expression of pride: Evidence for cross-cultural recognition Journal of Personality and Social Psychology. 94(3): 516-530.

Urbaniak, Anthony. Nonverbal communication in selling. SuperVision[Burlington]. 2005. 66(6): 13-15.

Van Baaren, R. B., R. W. Holland, K. Kawakami, and A. van Knippenberg. 2003. Mimicry and pro-social behavior. Psychological Science 15: 71-74.

Van Swol, L. M. 2003. The effects of nonverbal mirroring on perceived persuasiveness, agreement with an imitator, and reciprocity in a group discussion. Communication Research 30 (4): 461-480.

Van Swol, L. M. 2003. The effects of nonverbal mirroring on perceived persuasiveness, agreement with an imitator, and reciprocity in a group discussion. Communication Research 30 (4): 461.

Vargas, M. F. 1986. Louder Than Words: An Introduction to Non-Verbal Communication. Ames, Iowa State University Press.

Vargas, Marjorie Fink (1986). Louder than Words: An Introduction to Nonverbal Communication (Ames:

Vrij, A. 1997. Individual differences in hand movements during deception. Source: Journal of nonverbal behavior. 21: 87-102.

Vrij, A. and G. R. Semin. 1996. Lie experts' beliefs about nonverbal indicators of deception. Journal of Nonverbal Behavior 20: 65-80.

Vrij, A., S. Mann, and S. Kristen. 2007. Cues to deception and ability to detect lies as a function of police interview styles. Law and Human Behavior 31 (5): 499-518.

Vrij, A.. 2004. Why professionals fail to catch liars and how they can improve Source: Legal and Criminological Psychology. 9:159-181.

Vrij, Aldert, Gün R. Semin, and Ray Bull (1996). "Insight into Behavior Displayed During Deception." In Human Communication Research (Vol. 22, No. 4), pp. 544-62.

Vrij, Aldert, Lucy Akehurst, and Paul Morris (1997). "Individual Differences in Hand Movements During Deception." In Journal of Nonverbal Behavior (Vol. 21, No. 2), pp. 87-102.

Vrugt, Anneke, and Ada Kerkstra (1984). "Sex Differences in Nonverbal Communication." In Semiotica (50-1/2), pp. 1-41.

Walker. 1983 The expressive function of the eye flash. Journal of nonverbal behavior. 8(1): 3 - 13.

Walters, Mark Jerome (1988). Courtship in the Animal Kingdom (New York: Doubleday).

Watson KK, Matthews BJ, Allman JM 2007. Brain activation during sight gags and language-dependent humor. Cereb Cortex 17(2): 314–24.

Watson, N. V., & Kimura, D. 1991. Nontrivial sex differences in throwing and intercepting: Relation to psychometrically-defined spatial functions. Personality and Individual Differences. 12: 375–385.

Webster, Dan (2000). "Clothes Call." In Spokesman-Review (April 15), pp. E1, E10.

Wickelgren, Ingrid (1998). "The Cerebellum: The Brain's Engine of Agility." In Science (Vol. 281, No.

Wiener, Norbert (1950). The Human Use of Human Beings: Cybernetics and Society (New York: Avon Books), 1971.

Wild, Gaynor C. and Edward C. Benzel (1994). Essentials of Neurochemistry (Boston: Jones and Bartlett).

Williams. 1993. Effects of Mutual Gaze and Touch on Attraction, Mood, and Cardiovascular Reactivity Source: Journal of Research in Personality. 27(2): 170-183.

Willis, F. 1966. Initial speaking distance as a function of the speaker's relationship. Psychonomic Science. 5: 221-222.

Willis, F. N. (1966). "Initial Speaking Distance as a Function of the Speaker's Relationship." In Psychonomic Science (Vol. 5), pp. 221-22.

Willis, F. N., & Hamm, H. K. 1980. The use of interpersonal touch in securing compliance. Journal of Nonverbal Behavior. 5: 49-55.

Willis, William D., Jr. (1998C). "The Somatosensory System." In Robert M. Berne and Matthew N. Levy (Eds.), Physiology (Ch. 8, New York: Mosby), pp. 109-28

Willis, William D., Jr. (1998D). "The Autonomic Nervous System and Its Central Control." In Robert M.

Willis, William D., Jr. (1998E). "Spinal Organization of Motor Function." In Robert M. Berne and Matthew N. Levy (Eds.), Physiology (Ch. 12, New York: Mosby), pp. 186-99.

Willis, William D., Jr. (1998F). "The Nervous System and Its Components." In Robert M. Berne and Matthew N. Levy (Eds.), Physiology (Ch. 6, New York: Mosby), pp. 81-96.

Willis, William D., Jr. (1998G). "The Visual System." In Robert M. Berne and Matthew N. Levy (Eds.), Physiology (Ch. 9, New York: Mosby), pp. 129-53.

Wilson P, R. 1968. Perceptual distortion of height as a function of ascribed academic status. The Journal of social psychology. 74: 97-97.

Wood, John Andy 2006. NLP revisited: nonverbal communications and signals of trustworthiness. Journal of Personal Selling & Sales Management. 26(2): 197.

Young, J. Z. (1978). Programs of the Brain (Oxford: Oxford University Press).

Zald, D. H. The human amygdala and the emotional evaluation of sensory stimuli. Brain Res. Brain Res. Rev. 2003. 41: 88–123.

Zweigenhaft, R. L. 1976. Personal space in the faculty office: Desk placement and the student-faculty interaction. Journal of Applied Psychology 61 (4): 529-532.

CPSIA information can be obtained
at www.ICGtesting.com
Printed in the USA
LVHW101153110622
720769LV00004BA/421